Breathing in Ashes

Breathing in Ashes

A Story of Hope in the Midst of Suffering

Kim Gunderson

Because of Emma...my gift of hope

For the Savior...my Giver of hope

CONTENTS

"By faith, Abraham, when called to go to a place he would later receive as his inheritance, obeyed and went, even though he did not know where he was going. By faith he made his home in the promised land like a stranger in a foreign country; he lived in tents, as did Isaac and Jacob, who were heirs with him of the same promise. For he was looking forward to the city with foundations, whose architect and builder is God."

Hebrews 11:8-10

Acknowledgements

"Therefore, encourage one another and build each other up, just as in fact you are doing." 1 Thessalonians 5:11 (NIV)

There are many people in my life who have lived out the truth of this verse...those who I've listed and many more who are not. People encouraged me to share my story and journeyed with me over the past several months as I wrote. Mom & Dad, thank you for believing in me...for always encouraging me to follow my dreams and never telling me I can't. Kevin...I'm so grateful you're my brother and my friend. Thank you for your sense of humor and helping me stay balanced. Dawn... you've got a good man! Thanks for sharing him, and being a part of our family. Larry & Kate...while you may be "in-laws", you're my true family.

Thank you...to those who've set about the task to specifically pray over the past months: Gretchen, Shana, Amy N., Cindy, Bonnie, Jill, Chad, Angee, Judy, Mom, Courtney, Julie, Sue, Don, Amy, Erin— thanks for interceding for me through this journey. Bryan—you're an incredible artist! You revealed my heart and story through such a beautiful cover. Kaye and Angee...your eye for detail and those hours listening to me verbally process are evident throughout this book. The family at Christ Community...for supporting & praying for my family as we've learned to live life without Emma into our new normal. Thank you for being a safe place to learn and grow, to cry and laugh, and above all, to worship our Heavenly Father together.

Bonnie, Jill & Cindy...I couldn't ask for better friends than the three of you. Thank you for walking with me through the valley, for sharing laughter and tears and intense sorrow, for holding up my arms when I was too engulfed in grief to do it myself. Matt & Dana, thanks for letting me step into your lives even when you wished for something different. We've come a long way. Kelsey...I learned so much from being your mom...we've certainly grown up together! Thanks for the ways you encourage me from your hugs and *I love you's* to your gift of coffee in the middle of the day to simply hanging out together. I love you bunches! My husband, Bill...thanks for allowing me to share our story...I love you. And Emma, thank you so much for being my stinkerpot and helping my dream come true. I miss you and still love you bigger than the universe.

Above all thank you, Jesus, for being near to the brokenhearted and binding up my wounds. Thank you for entrusting me with Emma—her life and death—so the world might know. I pray you will be honored and glorified through the words in this book. Without You, I am nothing.

PROLOGUE

"Whoever survives a test, whatever it may be, must tell the story. That is his duty." Elie Wiesel

This book you hold in your hands is the fulfillment of a dream. A dream to write, to be published. Ever since I can remember, I've taken pen in hand to create logic and sense by linking together letters and words. The feel of the pen in my fingers, as letters formed words and words became sentences, brought comfort. It allowed me to put into black and white the thoughts and feelings that rattled through my mind, to learn, to process, to grow.

Years have passed and the desire to write has increased. I've written insights and lessons, stories for kids, shared thoughts through emails. Simple ideas, sometimes ramblings, but I've always wondered: did I have *it*? That one thing I could share, that was unique to me? My story? My contribution to the world? "I want to be a part of the rescue team for our tired, overcrowded planet. The rescuers will be those people who help other people to think clearly, and to be honest and open-minded." (Pipher, Mary: Writing to Change the World, 5. New York: Penguin Group, 2006.) Sure, I've written curriculum and devotions, lesson plans and journals...but I wanted something more. I wanted to share that burning batch of words inside that just had to be written, no matter what...to teach...to inspire. "Writers are people who care enough to try to share their ideas with other people." (Pipher, Writing to Change the World, 8.)

Enter...my family. Bill and I married in 1997. Two single parents joined together, created an immediate family of five. Drama began right away—Bill suffered a massive stroke three short months after we said, "I do". Really tested the whole "in sickness and in health" thing. Blending three children with two step-parents wasn't a walk in the park either. Add major health crisis and you've got a recipe for disaster. Frustrations mounted. Arguments ensued. Yet somehow, in spite of it all, we kept moving forward...together.

A new year arrived and with it much desired good news—a baby of our own to complete our blended family. The baby's name? For some reason, we only agreed on a girl's....Emma. Emma Jo. Named for Jane Austen's character and a few relatives, our baby-to-be would be a gift to each of us.

Emma was born on January 15, 2000, a couple of weeks early. From the beginning, she was a fun and easy baby. Emma belonged to all of us. She brought joy and laughter, from her toots and giggles to her huge hugs and smiles. She filled our home with love. Through all my dreams of writing, though, I never saw the storm coming—the sweep of death—that would roar into our lives and change us forever, causing Emma's sweetness to live on only in memory instead of reality.

This book is about another dream, too. A parent's worst nightmare. A reality that no one wants to live, a club no one chooses to join, a dream that should only occur when asleep. This nightmare raged into our lives, consumed every thought and feeling; threatened to pummel all sense of normalcy to the core of our very existence. Unannounced, unasked for, and at times unbearable, it almost destroyed all we held dear, its fingerprints left on the most precious of lives.

But life didn't stop with devastation. In time, suffering blended into hope, pain into redemption and trust led to faith, even without a happy ending here on earth. Life in our family continued on, but with a tender bittersweet thread forever entwined in our hearts as Emma now dances before the King in heaven instead of the middle of our family room floor.

I invite you in to see the other side of suffering—the thoughts and wrestling, the attempts to breathe, even amongst the ashes. Journey with me through the depths of a mother's fear and suffering. Someone once said that I've made suffering look easy. Suffering isn't easy. I've struggled, and continue to, some days more than others. I've questioned and wondered but chose to trust God and believe the depths of Jesus' love for me. Unfathomable love that I'd never have experienced had I not suffered, not allowed Him to work deeply in my heart and soul. I invite you to see the struggle behind the faith, the pain behind the smile, and the shattered heart that yearns for healing but won't be truly whole until I stand before my Savior.

But know this is my story, the way I remember the events that happened. This is the way I have grieved and suffered and attempted to honor God and my daughter through this nightmare. No two people grieve the same. Bill and I both lost Emma, for example, but we've grieved in our own ways, in our own time.

Look beyond the words and story for a glimpse of the power and hope in the midst of life that is available through a relationship with Jesus Christ. If you already know Jesus, my prayer for you is to be inspired, encouraged, and perhaps even challenged to prepare you for those times of suffering. They're there. Scripture is clear. It's not *if* we face trials of many kinds...but *when* (James 1:2). Your trial may look completely different than mine; that's to be expected. But the same God who led me through the darkness of the valley desires to be your guide, too.

If you don't know Jesus, please keep reading. Don't get stuck on religious talk or points that may not make sense to you, may not be totally clear.

Read on and allow yourself to be drawn into the story, an unbelievable story with a truly incredible Author. And I don't mean me....I mean Jesus, the true Author and Perfecter of life (Hebrews 12:2). Join me on this journey, breathe in with me and open your heart to new possibilities.

Chapter 1
The Fire

"Nothing is as far away as one minute ago." Jim Bishop

Who'd have thought a toy could save a life. An inanimate object, one that doesn't think or move or breathe. And not just any toy, a doll...one of Emma's favorite play things.

Emma loved her toys. Ponies and princesses. She'd set them up for countless hours of parties and swimming in the bathroom sink. Or maybe she gave them baths, I couldn't always tell. But I knew she had fun from the amount of time spent and water used. She would play for hours in the downstairs bathroom, just off the kitchen, with those dolls and ponies. Bare feet. Standing on tip toes stretching to reach the faucet. Stories unfolding in water adventures. Giggles bouncing throughout the house.

In a small way it seems right that a doll turned superhero that fateful morning; able to save a life through a single thought, a forgotten task, a moment of clarity.

This one toy, a child's simple plaything, transformed my life forever. If events had occurred just a little differently, I would've kept driving instead of turning around and returning home. One simple choice drastically altered my life...forever.

But I'm jumping ahead, scrolling faster than my fingers will type, will write, will tell this story of life, of death...of breathing.

On that morning, the doll became a superhero. The memory of her forgotten, sitting on a chair in our bedroom, led me back home to find my house in flames and the knowledge that my husband and my daughter might still be inside.

I'd turned my car around in an elementary school parking lot about a half mile from Christ Community Church, where I worked in children's ministry. It was just before that school when I remembered that doll...the super hero. I'd promised a co-worker she could borrow it to help teach an object lesson that Sunday. My car pointed home and I turned up the volume to continue to listen to a message by our senior pastor, Jim Nicodem, "For the Sake of the Neighbors".

A thought occurred to me as I drove: *God must really want me to hear this; to learn something about reaching those in my neighborhood.* I listened as he described a horrific situation: a house on fire,

but no one noticed. Firemen weren't available—
they were too busy hanging out at the fire station.
Neighbors didn't notice because they were too
caught up in their own lives. No one witnessed the
fire destroy someone's home.

At first the story sounded true. It was convincing.
No one around? No one noticed a house burning? Impossible. Surely someone saw it. Pastor Jim
then explained that the story wasn't true, not really. But there were people around us whose lives
were going up in flames. Did we notice?

I was hooked, engrossed as I turned into my subdivision, focused and prayerful. Wanting to learn...
to care...to see those around me, others in need.
I turned left...right...then left again. And that's
when I saw it.

The smoke.

Pouring from my house.

Unable to process the sight that unfolded before
my eyes the first thought swirled in my mind...*that's
not right. Smoke shouldn't be there.* My second
thought? *Where is everyone? Why isn't anyone
doing anything?* My third...*where's my daughter
and my husband?* It was Bill's day to be at home
with Emma, our youngest.

It'd been an early start that day. Getting our older two girls off to school—Kelsey to middle school and Dana to high school. The plan was to walk, shower, dress, then work.

For some reason I decided not to walk that morning. The need to get to work early outweighed the desire for fresh air. I could walk later, I reasoned. The doll was on my mind—the one I needed to bring in—not to forget it. Bill and Emma were still asleep in our bed. Emma scampered in sometime during the night, like usual. I leaned over my husband to kiss him goodbye. Usually it's a light kiss, so I wouldn't wake him. This time there was a need for him to be awake, aware that I was leaving. I talked with him, told him I was heading out. Then I glanced at Emma, not realizing that would be the last moment I saw her alive, breathing on her own. If only I'd known what was coming. I would've scooped her up, smothered her with a lifetime of kisses and hugs until she'd wriggle away from me, giggling, trying to catch her breath. Just like always. If only I'd known, so much would've been different.

But I didn't know. So I left. No hugs or kisses. No goodbyes. I just walked out of the room, focused on my day ahead, clothes in the dryer, a breakfast sandwich in my hand. A brief memory of a whiff of smoke, but being the overreactor, I chose to trust God that it would be nothing...nothing serious. I chose to trust, to believe that He was in control and would keep my family safe.

A mere fifteen minutes later, I pulled back into my driveway, thoughts of the forgotten doll lost to the sight before me. Smoke poured from our bedroom windows...from vents in the roof. Smoke seemed to leak from every possible opening in our house. I jumped out of the car and ran to the front door. I stopped, confused. Where was everyone? Gingerly I opened the door, unsure of what I'd see.

Nothing. Nothing out of the ordinary.

The sound assaulted me. The silence; it screamed. I closed the screen door and walked around the side of the house, uncertain. The smoke continued to billow from the front, filled the sky. All the while I wondered about Emma, curious where she and Bill were; waited to hear them call from our neighbor's house. *We've called the fire department— get away from the house!* Surely Bill would cry to me from their doorstep. Surely they were safe.

But there was nothing. Nothing but silence to keep me company. And the sound of my breathing... my heart pounding.

As I rounded the corner of the house, I saw it. The cause of the smoke. The beast. Flames reached from the grass to the tip of our roof, followed the line of the chimney. The family room? The fire raged and burned, destroyed my home, my sanctuary.

The silence screamed.

Reality slammed with a force that took my breath away. I was alone. No one was around. No one noticed my burning house. Just like the message I'd listened to. Shock gave way to fear. Fear became terror. In the middle crept a piece of knowledge that seized my breath once more.

Bill and Emma were still inside.

No one saw my house, the fire. No one knew there were two lives on the brink of death. I stood alone, not knowing what to do. Suffering barged in my life, unwelcome, unexpected, as I'd never experienced before.

I rushed to the front, realizing the worst. I called for Bill. I cried out for Emma. Nothing. Within seconds, or perhaps a lifetime, a man ran towards me. I called to him, "My husband and baby are still inside!"

Why did I call Emma my baby? She was five years old, hardly a baby anymore. And yet she was—the youngest, the baby of four. The one child Bill and I shared together. The one I wanted to protect, like a momma bear. Not that I didn't love or protect or care for Kelsey, or my step kids. But there was something different about Emma, something precious. We all felt it. Did we know somehow? Was there something in me that knew I'd only have her for a short while? That her life would end before mine? I have no idea, but I do know what words came out of my mouth—right or wrong. Emma was my baby, my precious gift, and she was caught inside of our burning house. Without me.

The stranger tossed me his cell phone and headed for the front door I'd left seconds before. Before he entered the house, I tried to dial 911. My hands shook uncontrollably. My fingers couldn't push the right buttons. I looked to this man, eyes wide, desperate. He took the phone, punched in the number and tossed it back. Somehow I caught this lifeline despite my trembling.

Seconds passed and the call was answered. What do I say in a moment like this? How would I explain the events that unfolded before me? Unbelievable words exhaled from my lips: *My house is on fire and my daughter and husband are inside.* My heart raced as terror became my companion. Somehow I remembered my address. My call was redirected to the local dispatch office. I repeated my reality. *My house in on fire and my daughter and husband are inside.*

Oh my...oh my God! I cried out to be heard. Would He listen? Would He answer the cry of a mother's heart? Emma and Bill were still inside! Flames crept down the hallway towards the front door and licked the roof of our porch. Smoke continued to pour from the house, billowing thicker, forced me to move back to safety. The lady on the phone asked if I wanted to keep talking as I waited for the firemen to arrive. I said I was okay and hung up.

Okay?! My husband and daughter were missing inside a burning building and all I could say was okay? I wanted to do something but felt frozen to the ground. Stuck. Screams caught in my throat, too deep to be released.

This wasn't the first time fire filled my heart with fear. But back then it wasn't real; it was only a thought... an idea...something unknown.

———

I suppose some details of life aren't necessary. Sure, they're facts and points of interest but significant to the movement of a story? Any story? My story? No, I don't think so. Not every detail needs to be shared. Knowing I was born in Cleveland, Ohio or that I have a brother, a mom & dad or that I'd lived in four different states by the time I was eight or had a pet growing up doesn't do anything to move the story along. Sure it's foundational kind of stuff, the basics, but significant? I guess an argument could be made that every piece of life history is important because it is the very history that makes me who I am today. But the specifics of where I went to school or what my childhood was like really don't bear any relevance to living life after the death of a child.

Occasionally however, there is a taste of foreshadowing that can only be appreciated when looking back. That moment in life that forewarns, that casts a spotlight, that doesn't make sense until the future becomes the present.

That childhood memory was but a taste of the horror yet to come. That first thought of the destruction of fire when I learned to breathe in the anxiety of its power, its potential to destroy the safety of my home. We'd just moved to St. Charles. I was in third grade. Our house was built to accommodate a family of six; we only had four. Two of their four kids lived in my room.

Why the details?

The red circles. There were two, stuck in the lower left corner of my window. The room was fairly large, a point I rather enjoyed since it was bigger than my brother's. An important distinction when you're only eight and your big brother liked to pick on you.

Their presence frustrated me, those two red stickers. Not so much because of their existence No, the presence of those two red circles weren't the issue; it was more the reason for their existence that caused anxiety.

Two red circle stickers on a window meant two children lived in that room. Important or an extraneous point? Important. Two circles equaled two kids, a fact firemen need to know in the event of a fire. A house fire.

My mother told me that one. Fire? Where I lived? Of course that would never happen to us. Would it? Someone apparently thought so; someone had been prepared. Those two red circles proved it, right there in the corner of my window.

Interestingly, about the same time we moved to St. Charles and those red dots taught me a distinctive life lesson, I received a Bible from my parents. My own Bible, the very first one I remember.....and inside the front cover was a gift from my mom, a verse, a promise from God.

Trust in the Lord with all your heart and lean not on your own understanding. In all your ways acknowledge him and he will direct your paths. Proverbs 3:5-6 (NIV)

This verse brought comfort to my eight-year-old heart. I could trust in Someone bigger than me. Whenever fear entered my mind, I could turn to God and know that He would protect me, lead me. Proverbs 3:5-6 taught me how to breathe when I was afraid. But somehow I missed a point—an important detail. In my innocence, or naivety, I thought if I believed the passage, if I trusted God, my life would go smoothly. Things would fall into place...because *I* trusted...because *I* did my part. Unfortunately, *I* also missed an important part of Proverbs 3:5-6...*and lean not on your own under-standing.* If I trusted God, then surely I'd know what was going on.

Yeah...right.

Why is it that we humans think that we can understand God's plan and purpose? That somehow, someway, we'd have the ability to understand His ways? Perhaps it's pride, or arrogance. I don't know. At eight, I think it was me being just that..... eight. I had a lot to learn. That verse became reality as I stood on the sidewalk of my house, watching it burn, knowing Bill and Emma were somewhere inside.

———

The man, that Good Samaritan, had gone in the house a couple of times in search of my precious daughter and husband. The second time he came out, he had news. *I felt your husband's foot. He's to the right of your front door. The dining room.* My husband? Good, that meant Emma was nearby. With that, he took a deep breath and plunged back into the inferno. Seconds later, he was at the door again, this time with Bill's body in tow.

I ran to hold the door open as he dragged Bill feet first out of the house. His body limp, like a rag doll Emma used to carry. Blood poured from his arm. His eyes open, glazed with the glimmer of death. CPR was administered immediately. A puff of smoke escaped Bill's mouth. Dark, almost black, just like the kind pouring out of my house. The thought that ran through my head? *This is what my husband looks like dead.* My next thought screamed: *EMMA!*

I caught a glimpse of death peering from Bill's face before. Three months after we were married, Bill suffered a massive stroke which, according to doctors, *took out the left side of his brain.* The neurologist said that Bill would either die or be a vegetable. No other options. Death stood near. But this doctor didn't know God, or His plan. Bill survived.

But now it was Emma, our precious 5 year old, our gift...the one who tied our family of six together. The unraveling began. I dropped to my knees. The air was warm but the driveway still cold, a patch of ice clung to the sidewalk. On my knees I cried out to the One whom I knew was in control. *Please help him find Emma!* I begged God. *Please find Emma. Please find Emma.* A warm hand settled on my back. My Good Samaritan joined me in prayer before he continued his search for my baby.

At some point another man showed up. He pulled Bill further away from the house as the Good Samaritan entered that fiery furnace one more time, in a desperate search for Emma. This second man, whom I later learned was an off-duty fireman, instructed me to move my car so the ambulance could get close to the house. He continued to administer CPR to Bill while the search for Emma dragged on.

I backed my car into my neighbor's driveway knowing God was in control. Slowly people trickled out of their homes to face the reality of a house on fire, their neighbor's house. Someone they knew. A reality usually only heard about on the local news, not down the street.

I stood with the driver's door open as a thought slammed into my heart. *Emma's dead.* She'd been too long without oxygen, without the ability to breathe. I wanted to shove that thought away but couldn't escape it. Too many minutes had passed, from the time I left my house to when I stood by my car, watching as my life disappeared at the hands of this fire...I knew. My mother's heart knew that Emma was gone. I couldn't breathe.

Chaos ensued as the first fire trucks entered our street. People walked near, wanting to know what happened. I'd heard the sirens in the background, the first noise that registered in my mind. As I watched and waited, I made the type of calls no one wants. I tried to call my parents...no answer. The message I left was the worst. *My house is on fire and they can't find Emma.* I tried to call Christ Community, to reach someone. No answer. It hadn't dawned on me that it was too early for anyone to be there. Finally, I thought to call my boss, Larry Breeden, on his cell phone. He picked up my call and I said the words again. *My house is on fire and they can't find Emma.* Shock raged through the phone. Larry apologized and asked me to repeat myself, unable to absorb my words. So I did. *My house is on fire and they can't find Emma.* I don't remember hanging up.

My next call was to a good friend, Jill, who worked with me in children's ministry. Tears strangled my voice as I asked her husband to speak with her. Those dreaded words left my mouth; I hated each syllable. *Emma's dead. My house is on fire.*

The next moments continued in a blur, like a series of photographs, still action shots. Becky, my neighbor whose house should've been the sanctuary for Bill and Emma, ran towards me, screaming... crying out for an answer to the destruction developed before her. I told her Emma was still inside. Terror. *Click.* Fire truck after fire truck arrived, blocking any hope for a car to leave our neighborhood. *Click.* Seven fire stations in all. Seven towns. *Click.* Two ambulances, one pulled into our driveway, the other parked on the street. *Click. Click.* A guy slipped on that random patch of ice and fell. *That's gonna hurt,* I randomly thought, not realizing he was my Good Samaritan. *Click. Click. Click.* I watched as the firemen spread across our lawn like ants, determining the best way to enter. Ladders set up, reached our second story bedroom windows, firemen cautiously climbed through and entered the smoke-filled house. *Click. Click. Click. Click. Click. Breathe.......*

My dad showed up; he'd gotten the message I left. I turned, saw him walk towards me and darted towards him as fast as I could, somehow thinking that he'd make it all okay, that he'd make it right and keep the pain and reality away. As I ran into his arms, my precious Emma was carried out in another's. She'd been found and rescued from the fiery furnace, taken towards the waiting ambulance. But I didn't see her then. I have no memory of Emma at the house or linked directly to the fire. No visual stamp etched in my mind of her limp body cradled by a fireman. My focus was on my dad, allowing the strength of his arms to fend off the absolute horror that encased my heart.

Together, my dad and I walked back towards my car, waited, wondering what would happen next. Someone walked over to me and explained the ambulances were ready to take Emma and Bill to the local hospital. We needed to leave, to go there. The thought passed through my mind: *why are they taking Emma to the hospital? Didn't she die?* So I asked, hesitant to trust the tiny whisper of hope: *Is Emma alive?* The only response: *her heart is beating.*

Hope sprang like a quick growing plant. Could Emma possibly survive? Will she be okay? And Bill? I thought I remembered a lot from that morning but even now, different memories flash in my mind, memories that don't seem to fit in the right order. Like finally hearing the smoke detectors. Silence screamed at me when I'd first arrived but later all I could hear was the piercing whine of those smoke detectors. After a meeting with the fire investigator the following week, he assured me they'd been blaring the entire time. My senses had shut down in order to survive.

Firemen continued to fight the blaze that destroyed our home as we drove to the hospital. Memories of the ride blur together; it seemed to take forever and yet was over in a matter of minutes. I walked in the familiar emergency room. My name barely left my mouth before they ushered me inside. The ER buzzed with activity. Chaos followed me.

The snapshots continued. People started to show up at the hospital. My mom arrived. *Click*. A few people from church. *Click. Click*. A friend's sister who happened to work there. *Click*. I wore my sunglasses instead of my regular glasses, unable to see without them. *Click*. I asked Jill to get them from my car despite the sight she'd see as the fire-fighters still battled the blaze.

Some pictures were clearer than others. Seth, our children's ministry leader at the time, leaned against a wall, looking a bit out of place, unsure of what to do. What is protocol when an employee's house burned and two family members stood at the brink of life and death? How does one respond? For some reason, at that moment, it struck me funny. A moment of comic relief. Not the belly laugh kind...the kind that said *this was so completely unbelievable. Unrealistic. Unexpected. But you're here. Thank you. I can't process it all and I don't even know how to react*...but there he stood, ready to do whatever was needed. A reminder I wasn't alone, someone stood with me.

There was the moment I saw my mom, whom I tried to call earlier but couldn't reach her. I cried out: *It's happening again!* Death stared at me once more, this time it wasn't through Bill's stroke; it was in the face of my youngest daughter.

A nurse walked by and asked if I wanted to see Emma. I did. I walked towards the trauma room where doctors and nurses battled for Emma's life. One thought filled my mind: *What will I see?* I'd seen my house. The smoke. The fire. Emma had been inside. What did that mean for her body? Did fire do its damage to her tender skin as it'd burned holes through the walls of my house? Would I recognize her? Had the heat caressed her face? The words that cried inside my mind escaped in a breath. *Is she burned?*

The nurse looked at me. *Didn't anyone tell you? No burns. We can't find any on her.*

Relief filled my core. No burns. Fire hadn't laid a finger on my little girl's precious body. Heart racing, breathing labored, I stepped in the trauma room and saw Emma for the first time since I'd left for work less than 45 minutes earlier. Tubes protruded from her. People surrounded her, frantically tried to save her life. Soot covered her skin. But it was Emma. Whole. Untouched.

Shock held me to my place on the floor. I didn't want to get in the way of the heroes who worked diligently, scrambling about the room. Could she really live? My mind cried out...YES! My heart's desire....YES! But reality? She wasn't moving. A machine helped her breathe. I yearned to touch her, to hold her, to keep death as far away from her as possible. Fear filled me. I wanted to push every-one out, to be the only one in the room with her, the only one she needed. I needed to gather her in my arms and allow the sheer power of my love heal her, save her, breathe life into her. After all, wasn't I her mom? The one who pushed her into this world? What if she lived for a little while? What if her brain was damaged beyond repair? What if....she died? I stepped away.

Bill lay in the other trauma room; was he any bet-ter? His eyes closed; his body covered with the same soot. Black. Death. A machine breathed for him, too. What would I face in coming weeks? Two miracles? Two funerals?

People continued to arrive. How did they find out? Word spread as quickly as the fire that consumed my home. At one point I looked over and saw a police officer standing firm. How'd he know? My good friend Steve, from high school worked at the high school as a police liaison. He heard the news of the fire and picked up Dana and Kelsey, brought them to the hospital. I never even asked.

The kids. What would I tell them? Picture a slow mo-tion video. The tears. The crying. The need to be strong for them as I explained what I knew. *Some-how the house caught on fire. Your dad and Emma were inside. We're not sure if Emma will live.* As the words escaped my mouth, I realized my worst fear was upon me. My fear of losing a child. Not only the death of a child, but death by a house fire. Those two red circles were back, haunting me again.

———

I was the one who checked the smoke detectors in the house, made sure they worked, changed the batteries with the change of time. Any whiff of smoke and I prowled for the source. Limited candles, I hid the matches; did whatever I could do to keep our family safe.

Until now.

I'd smelled smoke that morning before I left. Not a lot, but a brief whiff, like a gentle kiss. I'd just cooked an egg sandwich for breakfast. Bill's voice filled my head as I caught that scent. *You always overreact. Nothing's gonna happen.* A moment of decision. Should I scour the house for the source of smoke or trust that nothing's wrong? I chose to trust. Because I did trust....I do trust. God has a plan and a purpose for my life (Jeremiah 29:11). Surely He knew my heart....knew my fears. He wouldn't allow me to experience more than I could handle. A death? A fire? I stood a moment longer. Breathed deep. No more smoke.

I'd been doing laundry that morning, too. My mom told me never to leave a washer or dryer unattended. A fire could erupt. But Bill was home, I reasoned. It was okay. He would wake up if something was wrong. So I left...trusted.

Is that what happened? Did I cause the fire because the dryer was left running? Or because I'd used the microwave? Was I to blame for the tragedy unfolding before me? Terror rooted deep in my heart. My breathing stopped, a moment forever suspended in my mind, burned deeply. *Was this my fault?*

Helicopters arrived to airlift Bill and Emma to a hospital near Chicago; one with a burn unit better equipped for circumstances such as ours. Kelsey, Dana and I, along with several others, stood at a window and watched Emma fly away to the other hospital, soon followed by Bill. I didn't know what to expect next. I didn't want to move. At that moment, a man walked into the ER. A moment of fleeting recognition. I walked towards him. *Were you at my house? Did you save my husband?* It was him, my Good Samaritan...Tony. It turned out he was the dad of one of Kelsey's friends, a neighbor.

Tony was also the one who'd slipped and fallen on that patch of ice. He was in pain, suffering from a shoulder injury, but his heart hurt more for us. I hugged him and whispered, *thank you*. He saved my husband. He risked his life for Emma. He was, and continues to be my hero.

Chapter 2
The beginning of the end

"Where there is love, there is pain." Spanish proverb

We needed to head out to Loyola. My boss, Larry, drove me and my best friend, Bonnie. Along the way I had to go...to the bathroom. How was that even possible? The worst moment of my life and my body betrayed me. How could basic functions continue when I might lose Emma? How could life seemingly move forward when mine screeched to a halt? How could I tell my boss to stop the car so I could go?

But I did. We stopped at a Holiday Inn. Such a weird moment forever etched in my mind alongside other useless memories. As Larry drove on toward our destination, to Loyola, I leaned my head against the cold window. Thoughts raced through my mind. Would Emma live? Would Bill? How would our family continue without all six of us at home? What was God doing in my life? How would I survive? I trusted Him but the fire still happened. Could I now trust Him with one of the most precious things in my life: could I trust God with Emma?

Larry, Bonnie and I were escorted up to the burn unit. People already waited, searching for information about Bill and Emma. The crowd grew so large that we were moved to a conference room, a room that became my home for the next 48 hours. One by one family members arrived. Some received a call and came right away. Others had been misinformed about the severity of injuries and didn't arrive until later. But eventually, we were all together.

Our senior pastor, Jim Nicodem, and executive pastor, Eric Rojas, arrived at the hospital at some point during the day. I wasn't sure what to say, to believe, to trust. Would these men have words of wisdom in light of the tragedy? Would they be able to tell me what to do? Help me know what to think? What to say? How to survive?

The moment of truth came midday. The doctor, the head of the burn unit, began with Emma. *The little girl*...that's what he called her. Not Emma, not your daughter...*the little girl. There's nothing we can do for her.* I continued to listen as he explained what was wrong, that Emma's brain had gone too long without oxygen. Her heart beat but there was nothing else. No reflexes. No reaction in her beautiful hazel eyes. Emma was brain dead. They would wait 24 hours to be sure, but if she didn't go into cardiac arrest within those 24 hours, they'd remove her from life support the next day.

In a moment of clarity I asked, *do I need to make that decision?* Fear gripped my heart and I held my breath. I didn't want that responsibility. I didn't want to make that decision...to turn off the machines. *No,* the doctor replied. *That's my job. I'm the doctor, not you. I'll make that call.* His words were like a balm to my shattered heart. I exhaled, just a bit. But reality settled in—Emma was dead. I'd known that truth at our house, but to hear the words...I couldn't breathe.

Then he talked about Bill. I learned he had third degree partial burns on both legs that would require skin grafts; the severity of his lung injury from breathing in super-heated air; the threat of pneumonia and infection. His chances were good, the doctor said, but he had a long road ahead.

Bill would live. Emma would die. My heart crumbled. I wanted to be grateful that Bill would survive, and I was. But how could I live in light of Emma's death? How would my mom's heart survive? I looked at Jim, my Senior Pastor, and asked *how do I do this?* My worst fear now reality. My child. Dead. I didn't know what to do, how to respond. His words? *I don't know.*

Neither did I.

———————

A few years earlier a family at church lost their little boy to cancer. The mom and I had attended a conference together. On the drive back, she shared how she felt, her struggles, her fears of life without her son.

After that conversation I begged God, *please don't ever ask me to lose one of my kids. Please don't let one of them die before me. It will kill me. Destroy me. They'd have to bury me, too.* I saw the pain in this mother's eyes, the suffering, the nightmares after her son died and the reality that life continued on without him. It scared me.

Apparently, God had other plans. My greatest fear stretched out before me.

How would I tell my kids? How would I tell my husband, once he woke up? How would I live without my Emma? Questions filled my mind. All questions, no answers.

I walked back to that conference room, steps slow. The doctor already told those who waited. I don't remember that. But I do remember the pattern of the carpet. Blue and red. Swirly. An odd pattern. Kind of ugly. Staring down as I walked, the need to speak truth out loud overwhelmed me. *I will not deny God. I will not deny God.* I said it to whoever would listen. My mom. Others in the hallway. It didn't matter. In that moment I made a choice, the choice to trust God...that He was in control. He knew what happened. While the fire and Emma's death came as a shock to me, it didn't catch Him off guard. He wasn't surprised. Somehow, in His infinite wisdom and plan, this all made sense. And I would trust Him even though I didn't get it, or like it, or knew where I would go or how I would survive. I would trust.

This was my Rachel moment. In 1999, a high school student from Columbine, Colorado faced the most definitive moment of her life. With a gun held to her head, death a very real possibility, the gunman told her if she denied God, he'd let her live. She refused. And she died.

I often pondered Rachel's decision. *What would I do in a moment like that? If a gun was held to my head, would I deny God in order to live?* I didn't have a gun pointed at me that day in the hospital but I felt it was the same, my Rachel moment. Death and fear stared me in the eye, my nightmare made real...what would I choose?

I suppose it would've been easy to say no, to blame God, to cry out to Him: *this isn't fair!* And it's not, from our perspective. A little girl was about to take her last breath. The one child in our family who belonged to each of us, who was the joy of my heart and her father's little buddy, her bestest sister's playmate, loved by all.

But I couldn't do it. I couldn't deny Him. I couldn't turn my back on the One who gives me life and breath....who actually gave Emma to us. I refused to deny Him, just like Rachel.

That decision not to deny God was a turning point for me. I believe, especially looking back from four years of distance and healing, that single decision allowed God direct access to my heart and my mind. I chose, in my worst moment, to believe that His Word was true, that He had a plan and a purpose not only for my life, but for Emma's as well.

I also believe at that moment I turned the page on Satan's schemes. His goal is destruction. "The thief comes to kill, steal and destroy." (John 10:10a) He wanted my biggest fear to emerge so I would crash and burn; so I would disown God and invalidate my life, my ministry, my relationship with Jesus. I refused to let him win. I chose to believe the second part of John 10:10—"The thief comes to kill, steal, and destroy. *But I have come that they may have life, and have it to the full.*" Full life, even in the midst of death. Emma's death.

Still the pain was so intense I went numb. Ever felt that? Stubbed your toe and, for a moment, the white-hot pain disappeared but you knew it would return…and it would hurt, a lot. Multiply that feeling by infinity and you might get a taste of the pain of losing a child.

At that moment, though, I hadn't lost her, not yet. It wasn't final, not completely. I could still see her, stroke her hair, watch her chest rise and fall…even if it was by a machine. I walked back to the conference room and repeated what we'd just learned. *Bill's going to be okay. Third degree burns. Serious lung injury. But Emma, she's not going to live.* Even as I said it, my heart shattered again. None of it mattered. Nothing mattered except Emma. I would never hold her again; never hear her voice or her laughter. Never again would I see her play with her ponies or listen to her giggle with her sisters. I would never feel her fingers run through my hair as sleep claimed her. Emma's short life was over.

Chapter 3
Fear of Death

"You gain strength, courage and confidence by every experience in which you really stop to look fear in the face. You must do the thing which you think you cannot do." Eleanor Roosevelt

Fear has always followed me, haunted me. Not the "what if there's no toilet paper" kind of fear, or "will my friends like my new outfit", or even "will we have enough money to make it this month" variety. Terror. Deep darkness. Fear of death. A life alone, without family, without loved ones. Nightmares plagued me about my parents' death—it didn't matter if it were my mom or my dad, sometimes even my brother. Dreams of death and then to wake with a tear-soaked pillow. As a young child I would steal into my parents' room, to see if what I had seen in my mind was real. Did she die? Was he still alive? I had to see them, breathing. Standing on my mom's side of the bed...afraid to wake my dad...I'd touch her shoulder. She'd wake, ask what was wrong. I'd cry. *You died*. She'd hug me; walk me back to my room and then rub my back and tell me everything was okay. It was just a dream.

Only Emma's death wasn't a dream. And my mom couldn't tenderly soothe away my fears, the sadness, the tears. This time it was real. And it was my child who died.

Why did death scare me? Fear of the unknown? The separation? The uncertainty? Sure, I knew there was a heaven. As a child I'd heard about it in Sunday School. Jesus lived there. But it felt so far away. Unreal. Other people went there. I knew I'd go one day, but honestly, as a young child, I didn't want to because it meant living without people I loved here on earth.

Was it because of my deep love for my family? Because of the amount of change I went through as a kid—living in four different states, not having the same people in my life? Friends constantly changing?

Honestly, I don't know.

But the fear was real...and I didn't know how to get past it.

When I first heard of death—that people left this earth and didn't stay forever, we lived in New Jersey; I was about five. A young neighbor girl from Cleveland had died. She was just a little older than me. *What's death?* I asked my mom. *When someone isn't here anymore. She's in heaven.* What a foreign concept for a five year old. Not here? Without her mommy and daddy? That sounded scary. My little five-year-old mind tried to reason, to understand. All I took away was the terror of being alone.

It was quite a while until death touched my life again. During grade school, a young woman from church, the daughter of my mom's good friend... Sheri, was killed in a car accident. Death whispered once again. Where was she? How would her mom survive? Sitting near the window in my bedroom, that one with the red circles, I cried. *God, why did you let her die? What about her family? Her mom? Her husband? The baby she was carrying?* Only quietness answered.

Then came the summer after my senior year of high school. A gentleman whom I affectionately called my Illinois grandfather, Wes, died of cancer. A man who loved God. He sang "The Old Rugged Cross" in church. How he would sing! His rich baritone voice filled the entire building, almost as if he desired to reach God in heaven itself simply with his the sound of his voice. But it was the tears I remember as he sang the lyrics. *I will cling to the old rugged cross, and exchange it one day for a crown.* Exchange the pain, the suffering...with joy, God's presence. He cried every time he sang those words. Back then I wondered why.

Now I know.

Still the question rattled around in my mind: how could not being here be better? My eyes only saw the pain, the loss. I didn't look beyond this world. My eyes and focus stayed here on this life. I didn't want to feel the sorrow. I didn't want to lose a person I loved.

After Wes died, I did attend the funeral, the celebration of his life. And it truly was a celebration. His grandson spoke of his love for Jesus. His son spoke of his desire to be with Jesus. Sure there were tears, but there was joy. Joy because Wes was in heaven.

I didn't feel joyful. I felt sad. I'd never see him again and I refused to go to the front and see his body. I couldn't. I wanted to remember what he looked like alive. Healthy. Singing. So I didn't. I left the church without a final goodbye, without one last look.

Now I wonder what he looks like...or rather I wonder how he sounds. How he's singing to his King having exchanged his cross for a crown. Maybe Emma stands beside him, singing, too. Her small hand grasping his.

Without me.

That's one part of death I struggle with, I think, a part I hate: the pain and suffering associated with death. Even though Emma didn't suffer long, if at all. One fireman explained that the house was so hot the family room flashed. Everything burned, including the air. It would've taken about three breaths of the super-heated air to knock her out, her little lungs overwhelmed with intense heat. But there are others, those who die slowly whether it from cancer eating away at their bodies or other diseases that slowly take over, replacing healthy cells with sickly ones. The pain. The suffering. The hurt. The lack of ability to *do* something for them. Yes, that part is definitely difficult.

I guess it's even more than that, though. It's the separation. Not being able to see Emma any more. I can't hear her or watch her grow. I can't tickle her or have her try and tickle me back. No more love wars: *I love you bigger than a chocolate chip cookie. I love you bigger than a hangaber (Emma translation: hamburger).* Back and forth we'd go. I miss saying those words. I miss blowing "zerberts" on her belly...those raspberries that brought giggle after giggle escaping from the depths of her toes. Oh how I long to hear that sound.

I did finally see a dead body; the only other time before seeing Emma. I was totally freaked out. It was lifeless...cold...hard. The mom of my best friend from high school died just after I graduated from college. Someone I knew. She'd been sick for a long time. On one hand it seemed okay, her mom wasn't hurting anymore. No more sickness or pain. No more inflated donuts to sit on because of a boil on her fanny. No more frail cries for her daughter…"L.a.u.r.a." Every time she called out my friend flinched. What would it be this time?

And yet when her mom died, there were great tears. This was her *mom*. The one who gave her life, who took care of her as a child, who looked out for her, or at least was supposed to. The separation was final, over, never to be seen again on earth. There was pain…deep sadness…uncertainty.

It took everything in me to walk up to the casket, through the line and "pay my respects". I didn't want to see the "body". I didn't want to think of all the hours spent at her house, listening to her cluck her tongue or smack her lips, thirsty…or just vying for attention, now silent. I didn't want to look at what was left. What would go in the ground…the emptiness.

Death is final. No rewind on life's remote. No playback or erase. Separation. An end.

Or is it? Could there be something more? Something we can't see now but feel with our hearts; that resonates deep within our souls? Could we be longing for something more? "And we believers also groan, even though we have the Holy Spirit within us as a foretaste of future glory, for we long for our bodies to be released from sin and suffering. We, too, wait with eager hope for the day when God will give us our full rights as his adopted children, including the new bodies he has promised us." (Romans 8:23)

Is that why people can believe this world is all there is; because they don't feel there may be something more? Don't long for something better? Is it that they can't see it? Or may flat out refuse to believe God's Word to be true? I don't know if those who feel that way have ever lost someone to death. Perhaps they have—but is that comforting, believing that the person whom they loved no longer exists? Is nothing? Gone forever?

Hmmm...

I don't know. The thought that Emma no longer exists, that I'll never see her again is incredibly depressing and would make life...surviving...living without her completely unbearable. Impossible. I suppose I'd rather live with hope knowing I will see her again rather than imagining this life was it.

But many do feel hopeless. I get that because that feeling did live in my heart for a time.

Hopelessness...right after Bill's stroke. We'd been married a short three months when death stared us in the eye, up close and personal. It scared me beyond anything I'd experienced before. The feeling of emptiness formed crystal clear in my mind. Bill was home, he'd survived the initial stroke. As for his "quality" of life, we weren't quite so sure yet, or even if it would happen again. Uncertainty became our constant during that time. Often revisits, even now.

After his stroke, Bill spent a lot of time in rehab; learned how to talk and walk and use different tools to help him remember basic things. Like what to call an elbow, a lamp, or a watch. It seemed every hopeless thought crept in my mind in the morning. Maybe that's why I don't like mornings. Or perhaps it was because those were the only moments of quiet living in a two-bedroom townhouse with five people....three being kids. In those moments of silence I'd sit on the edge of the tub, thoughts of despair slunk in. What if? What if there was nothing beyond this world? What if death was the end? What if God was not real? Not powerful? Or simply didn't care? What if this really was it? I felt like I'd fallen into a black hole of nothingness. I was beyond scared. I was beyond terrified. Anxiety consumed me. Some have called it *the dark night of the soul*, that time of wrestling about God...His promises...His reality but sensing nothing except darkness.

This desperation pushed me towards the Bible, the only source of Truth I knew. Growing up I'd memorized a few verses, knew some of the stories. But I needed to know how it played out in "real" life. It'd been written so long ago. Was it real? Truly real, not just someone's imagination or the result of a bunch of people getting together to try and trick the world? Did it apply to my life? Could I truly trust it for answers and wisdom and knowledge?

I cried out to Him, just like David did as recorded throughout the Psalms: "O Lord, hear me as I pray; pay attention to my groaning." (Psalm 5:1) I trusted that He would hear me, even though my feelings told me otherwise. "As for me, I look to the Lord for help. I wait confidently for God to save me, and my God will certainly hear me." (Micah 7:7)

I'm not sure when the darkness began to clear. I kept seeking, kept asking, kept trusting. I tried to live out Proverbs 3:5-6, trusting God without leaning on my own understanding. Some days were better than others, some moments more apparent. Over time my trust grew and I could feel God listening...answering.

I think I learned to trust because even those feelings after Bill's stroke really weren't the first time I'd visited that place of despair. The search for understanding hadn't started then. There was a darker moment, a more desperate cry for help, a moment of reality. Kelsey and I lived in DeKalb, a couple of years before I'd met Bill. After college, I worked as a teacher for the hearing impaired. The year...1995. Something horrific happened in Oklahoma City. A bombing. Death. Destruction by "one of our own", on our own soil. A glimpse into the future?

It was night as I sat out on my patio after hearing of the tragedy. Kelsey slept as I tried to grasp the gravity of what had happened. The bombing was one of the first experiences my generation had with this level of destruction. Many people died because of one person's choice. And it wasn't just adults who had died, innocent children suffered. One particular picture haunted me.....a fireman tenderly carried a young child from the burning building. Foreshadowing? God's warning? Grace?

Perhaps. I just didn't know it at that moment.

But it scared me. The devastation scared me to the point of crying out to Him, seeking Him. Writing in my journal....*where are you, God?! I feel as lost and vacant as the blackness of the sky before the stars peek out. Nothingness. Are you there? Do you even care?*

The first dark night of my soul.

The second was after Bill's stroke.

The third was after Emma died...right?

Honestly, not really. Yes, it was dark but more because of the deep grief I felt for Emma than any distance from God. Perhaps it was because I'd found truth after emerging from those other two experiences, truth of God's faithfulness and His sovereignty—being in control no matter what happened in my life, or the world around me. I asked. I searched. I had to know if there was something more—even if I couldn't see it. "So we fix our eyes not on what is seen, but on what is unseen. For what is seen is temporary, but what is unseen is eternal." (1 Corinthians 4:18)

It was during those earlier moments as I sought God, wrestled with Him and learned about his faithfulness, regardless of how I felt, that gave me practice, so to speak, to endure the darkest moment of my life...Emma's death. That earlier time sitting on the patio of my apartment, alone, sad, unsure of God's presence...yes, that night was black. But something began to take root deep inside...faith. To believe in something I couldn't see. Hebrews 11:1 explains it this way: "Now faith is being sure of what we hope for and certain of what we do not see."

That's why I need to talk to God, to pray, to soak in the Source of life. I desperately cried out as David did—"My God, my God, why have you abandoned me? Why are you so far away when I groan for help? Every day I call to you, my God, but you do not answer. Every night you hear my voice, but I find no relief." (Psalm 22:1-2)

Not only could I not see the point in the death of innocent children, that night in 1995, but I couldn't even see God. His goodness…His power…where was it? I cried out to Him anyway. I stood firm and believed He was real, that He would hear me…. even though it didn't feel like he did. I chose to continue to seek Him, even though I couldn't see Him. To believe, even though the only proof I had was the evil that lived in this world, stirring in someone to make a choice to take the life of another, let alone many…including children.

This trust did not happened all at once; there was no single "ah ha!" moment in my life. Over time it felt more like a steady stream of desperately needed water, nourishing my soul rather than a fire hose threatening to drown me.

After Bill's stroke those feelings returned. Questioning…wondering….hoping. Surely there had to be something more. The emptiness I felt was overwhelming. The Bible had to be true. If the Bible wasn't, if this was it—the despair—then I didn't

want any of it. I'd rather take a step of faith believing that God's Word is true than believe in this
nothingness that I felt.

Perhaps those may not be the most theologically
sound explanations or arguments and there could
be a lot of questions here. My point? To ask and
talk to God. I chose to take God at His Word. All of
it. Not just some of it. I wrote out my questions and
struggles in my journals. I cried out. I kept reading,
kept pursuing. My heart needed to know there
was something more to this world, more than the
suffering and pain. And God showed me there
was.

But now it was Emma. My worst nightmare had
come true. Even though I was learning to trust
God with life, and death, it hadn't hit that closely
to home. Sure, the people I'd mentioned that I
knew and loved had died. My grandfather in 1993.
My uncle in 2003. But they lived in another state.
Death didn't touch my daily moments; I hadn't
seen it every day.

Until now.

Chapter 4
Decisions, Thoughts and Organ Donation

"You can close your eyes to the things you do not want to see, but you cannot close your heart to the things you do not want to feel." Anonymous

The next hours were spent waiting. Waiting to see Bill. Waiting for updates. Waiting for different family members to show up. Waiting to hear those dreadful words: *I'm sorry. Emma is gone.* No, not Emma...*the little girl.*

Even in the midst of the trauma, I saw evidence of God's goodness. The support from my family. Friends came, called, prayed; church set up 24-hour prayer to cover our family. People bought us clothes since we owned nothing but the ones on our backs. But one moment stands out above the rest; shone brightly and struck deeply.

Emma and Bill's rooms were across from each other in the burn unit. Emma's to the right, Bill's to the left. Honestly, I didn't spend a lot of time in their rooms at first. There was a lot to do, to figure out. I was scared, terrified, overwhelmed. Some have criticized me for that. But they've never faced it... the death of a child from such destruction; their husbands on the brink of death. They've never walked in my shoes so, to be blunt, they just don't get it.

The moment happened in Emma's room with my mom. There may have been others there, I honestly don't remember. But I do remember the squeeze. The feel of Emma's fingers wrapped around mine. I'd held her hand, stroked her tender skin, touched her hair; wished and prayed and begged God to perform a miracle. Her eyes closed, a breathing tube kept air flowing in and out of her lungs. We'd already been told there wasn't much hope.

But she squeezed my finger. I felt it. Okay, most likely Emma didn't make that choice. She couldn't. Her brain no longer worked. As tears ran down my cheeks, from sadness and hope, I told my mom *it's probably just a reflex, but I'll take it.*

What hadn't sunk into my mind was that when someone is brain-dead, they don't make choices....and they don't have reflexes.

None.

But Emma squeezed my finger. It was real. I can still feel the warmth and the pressure; the race of my heart as my precious little girl—and my loving Father—offered me the briefest moment of comfort.

I'll believe it. And remember it. Treasure it. And return to that memory in moments of desperation and darkness, when I wonder if God is really as good as His Word says.

He is.

And in that moment God's goodness was offered in the gentle touch of a little girl to her mommy.

I didn't want to sleep that night. I couldn't. I was afraid where my dreams might take me. Would I see those flames again as they consumed our home? Would Emma's face float before me? Disfigured from the fire even though she was untouched in reality? Would I scream in fear at the horror my life had become?

As the day ended, my parents took Kelsey and Dana home. Home...we had no home. They went to my parent's. Our oldest, Matt, had shown up at some point but left when they did. A few people stayed. Some close friends, Bonnie and Jill, Bill's sister and my boss, Larry. There may have been others but memories blurred together. We sprawled on the floor or lounged in the chairs in the conference room. I tried to sleep, curled up in a ball on the floor. Every time the door to the conference room opened, my heart raced. *This is the moment,* I told myself. I held my breath. *Emma is dead.* But it wasn't. Nurses checked on us. About 4 am that next morning Geri arrived, another friend. She drove all the way just to pray. Awake part of the night, she figured she could either pray at home, or be with me. She chose me.

The next day came...dreaded...unwanted. Time continued, no matter how much I wished it would stop. This was the day. People returned and more arrived. If I didn't know reality, I'd have thought it was a party. Only this party wasn't joyful. Or fun.

Around noon the doctor came to get me. It was time. There wasn't any more to do for *the little girl.* Oh how I wanted him to say Emma's name. *Emma!* I wanted to scream. *The little girl's name is Emma! She has a life...had a life! She was real and she was mine. She lived and breathed and moved...she wasn't just the little girl. Her name is Emma!* But he moved on, told me it was final. And then he wanted me to talk with someone. A lady who worked with something called Gift of Hope. At first I was unclear. Emma was dead. What did this lady want? Why would I need to talk with her about my daughter?

Organ donation. Every part of my being wanted to cry *NO! You can't take my little girl apart! You can't have any piece of her! Don't touch her. Please.* But reality set in. Emma didn't need her organs. She didn't need anything, not even me. I sat and listened as this lady offered her condolences. I listened as she explained the options, which organs could save a life, which ones could help someone live a better life, which ones could help science. I listened but screamed inside. Screamed for this nightmare to stop. Screamed to catch my breath, to process it all...for my Emma. Screamed on in silence.

Save a life. Only the organs that would save a life, allow someone else more moments to breathe. It was very clear to me. Not her eyes—I couldn't bear the thought knowing someone had her eyes, someone else looking at life through those beautiful hazel eyes. Both kidneys, liver, pancreas and her heart. To save a life. Five organs, five people...five years of her life. I prayed for those who received her organs...those pieces of Emma that would live on. I prayed they would realize the precious gift they received, the great sacrifice offered so they might live.

In a daze, I walked back to the conference room, that space that served as our waiting room. The waiting room...for what? Death? Loss? Suffering?

For Emma to leave me behind? For complete despair to consume me?

A former co-worker asked me how it went...what just happened. What just happened?! I signed away the wholeness of my daughter's body. The skin I touched and tickled and bathed. The space that filled my arms as I held her close.

Me. Emma's mommy...her protector...her caregiver. I signed a sheet of paper granting permission for a complete stranger to mutilate her precious body. To cut it open and remove pieces that brought life and breath, allowed her to function.

How could I let someone do that to her? To take a scalpel to her skin and slice? What kind of mother allowed someone to remove bits and pieces in hope that somehow, somewhere, a piece of her would live on...still operate...still survive?

In that moment my heart stood on the brink of survival. No, Emma didn't need her organs anymore. The logical part of my brain understood that. But someone did. Someone prayed for a miracle the same moment sorrow became my companion. A modern-day Jairus' daughter...or son...begging the same God I begged to allow Emma to live (Mark 5:22-24; 35-42).

Purpose. Signing those papers allowed a glimmer of purpose behind Emma's death. Or perhaps it was redemption. Not allowing death the final say. Victory. Five lives touched by my one precious daughter. A small snapshot within the bigger picture. Something good. *Click.*

But oh how my heart hurt. I wanted to be there as Emma drew her final breath. It didn't matter that a machine filled her lungs with air...that she couldn't breathe on her own. I wanted to hold her as she left this world and entered Jesus' presence. A small gift. My own gift of hope.

I wanted it. Selfishly, I wanted a link, to be the last one Emma touched before touching her Savior, my Savior. I craved it.

But it wasn't allowed. A stranger would do that. After stitching her closed. After turning off the machines that kept the air flowing through her lungs. I felt cheated. I was the one who brought her into this world! I had carried her in my body; felt every kick...laughed at every turn.

Not one of these thoughts became a spoken word. Only my pen and my journal knew of these feelings. And God. He heard me. "Evening, morning and noon I cry out in distress, and he hears my voice." (Psalm 55:17) And He held me as closely as I desperately wanted to hold my little girl. How could I have shared these thoughts with those in the room—the ones who still had all their children? Those who would be able to tuck their kids into bed that night while I waited for Emma to breathe her last? Would they have understood?

Don't get me wrong. In the midst of this rambling and sharing, there is no bitterness. Not even close. I wanted to touch hope. To feel the tangible, the reality of heaven…something beyond what is seen in this world. I believe in heaven and all its goodness. My heart just wanted to touch it…needed to embrace it.

It's the reality to which I felt cheated. Emma was heading to my heart's home. It felt so close…to see Jesus face to face. Holding her in those last moments would have let me feel like Thomas as he touched Christ's scarred hands. To touch! For real! To experience…for my faith to become sight (John 20:24-27).

It just wasn't my turn. It was Emma's. All I could do in that moment in the waiting room was wait. To breathe deeply: in…..out…in….out. Breathe in God's goodness and faithfulness. Breathe out the fear and sadness. Breathe in the hope that what God says in his Word is true; no matter if I'm breathing in ashes or the fresh wind of His love.

Chapter 5
Goodbye for Now

"The only way round is through." Robert Frost

The despised moment arrived too soon: the time to say goodbye to Emma, for now. Definitely not forever. My family stood around her bed, the only sound registered were the ventilator and the tears. An interesting combination.

My parents, Kelsey, Matt and Dana stood there, trying to figure out what to do. I think my mom prayed. Or not. I don't totally remember. What I do remember was the intense feeling of failure, that somehow I'd let Emma down, failed to protect her, to keep her safe. I didn't know how to say goodbye to my child. My heart knew she wasn't there, she wouldn't hear anything. That moment was for us. The ones left behind. But those words wanted to be said, shouted, proclaimed...heard. By Emma.

Somehow I had to say it. Goodbye. I whispered in her ear. For now. And *I'm sorry. Oh Emma, I'm so sorry I wasn't a better mommy to you. That I couldn't protect you from the smoke. That you're*

going on to a place I've never been, without me.
I didn't want to leave.

My mom and dad stood at the foot of her bed. Dad's hand on Emma's foot, gently shaking it... willing her to wake up. Not to be in *that* moment, the final one. I wanted to join him...to shout...to make God perform a miracle. By my sheer will I wanted Emma to open her eyes, to breathe on her own.

One by one we spoke. *Goodbye, Emma. I love you bigger than my pain, my shattered heart. Goodbye for now. I'll see you in heaven one day.* Even my dad said those words after some encouragement from my mom. A victory? Perhaps. But a bittersweet one. I really don't like saying goodbye.

I really don't like other people telling me what to do, either. A fault of mine, I know. I try. But in those moments, at that time...those decisions belonged to me. The one thing I could still do for Emma, for Bill. Until one of his friends showed up in the waiting room. And spoke truth; it just didn't feel that way at the time.

He told me I needed to wait to have the burial service for Emma.

Seriously?

Whatever. We'd just said goodbye to her. Services hadn't even been planned yet and the thought already went to the burial, to wait. Really? For how long? No one could answer because we didn't know. But we did need to wait. What if there ended up being another funeral? Prolonged suffering. As if life now wasn't hard enough.

But he spoke wise words, Bill's friend. I listened, chose to wait. It was the right decision. It allowed Bill a chance to see Emma's body, to process what had happened. Yet in that moment, right after saying Goodbye to her, it was the last thing I wanted to hear.

At some point the hospital social worker talked with my parents. He instructed them to take me home, to leave the hospital. Was he afraid I'd never leave if I didn't go then? Who knows, but I did need a break. And a shower. My clothes reeked of smoke. My fear produced a stench that I hadn't noticed till later. Barely twenty-four hours had passed since I first glimpsed the smoke pouring out of my home.

But they couldn't drive me home. I had no home.

As my parents and I walked out of the hospital, I noticed a painting in one of the hallways, just off the entrance to the parking lot. A painting of a pair of red shoes. No child, just an empty pair of shoes. That painting brought a fresh wave of sadness through my heart. I felt as empty as those shoes. I hated that painting.

I sank into the backseat of my dad's car, grateful and numb at the same time. Grateful for the comfort that supported my body, the quiet...no more beeping from machines. Numb because....well, just because. I'd never have to drive Emma anywhere again or care for her, or buy her clothes or toys or anything. Tears poured down my face. But in the quietness of that moment, despite the tears, I made a couple decisions.

I wanted to see Tony, my Good Samaritan. He'd been hurt; a shoulder injury from his fall on the ice had required surgery. I wanted to thank him.

I needed to go the store.

It's amazing what goes through our minds in those kinds of moments. But those were the things I wanted to do. Before anything else.

Chapter 6
So the World Will Know

"What can we do but keep on breathing in and out, modest and willing, and in our places?" Mary Oliver

My mom drove me to Tony's house, on the other side of our subdivision. We sat at their kitchen table, Tony with his wife, Annette. Me with my mom. We talked. I learned he had a relationship with Christ. It was his hand I'd felt on my back as I begged God to find Emma that first morning. He'd also forgotten something, not a doll but his cell phone... the very phone used to call 911.

I thanked him for pulling Bill out of the house. For searching for Emma. He had two daughters. He understood. But he didn't want thanks or any acknowledgement. He wanted things kept quiet, his part in it all.

He sure helped the wrong family!

I challenged him, as I'm known to do. The challenge was to honor God with his choice to save

Bill, to search for Emma. I asked him to share his story with whoever would listen so the world would know. Not to make it about me or Emma or Bill, or even him.

But about Jesus.

Every time I've questioned why Emma died or the fire happened, even now, that's the phrase that fills my mind. *So the world will know.* So others will hear the truth of Jesus' love for them. His own death and resurrection in exchange for our lives so we could have a relationship with his Father. People would listen. A child had died. Even the hardest of hearts would listen to that story. Wasn't that part of the message I'd listened to that fateful morning? *For the Sake of the Neighbors.*

Use it.

My mom and I left to go back to her house. And shower. To try and get rid of the smell of the fire. I washed my hair four times but the smell hung on. Clung to me. I hate that smell. Not the sweet aroma of burning leaves...but the acrid stench of destruction. The chemicals and our stuff mixed together through intense heat. Disgusting.

After I showered and changed, put on new clothes that didn't quite fit, weren't me at all, I asked my mom if I could use her car. One more objective. To shop.

As I walked into the store that first time I thought everyone would surely know what had happened, would be talking about it. The fire made the news. TV helicopters flew over our home as it burned. The story splashed across the front page of a couple different newspapers. First described the events of the fire, later said that Emma died. I've kept those papers. To remember where we've been so we can celebrate where we are and what God will do in the future.

But in that moment, in the store, I wondered if people saw me....a new grieving mom. A short few hours since the moment I'd said Goodbye. Was it written in my eyes? Plastered across my face? Would everyone know? Anyone see?

No. Life continued on as if the fire never happened. Because that's life. As much as suffering consumes our minds and our thoughts, the clock keeps ticking. Life still moves on, oblivious to the pain. People scurry about, unaware.

I thought I could handle being there, shopping. As soon as I stepped through the door, my heart raced with anxiety. Memories of Emma were everywhere. The red carts. The toys. The bathroom sign. A child crying. Feelings overwhelmed me. Tears threatened to spill. I chose what I needed and raced to check out. Prayed, hoped that no one would talk to me or ask me a question.

In the car the tears flowed. Sobs wracked my body. There I didn't care if anyone saw. Emma died. Bill was in a coma. I didn't care what anyone thought.

But I'd made it. I ventured into the world and then retreated to the security of a car. I took that first step. I often wonder if I hadn't done that, if I'd stayed away, if it'd been easier or more difficult to rejoin society. Would I have become a recluse? Afraid to engage in the world around me?

I returned to my parents' home, freshened up with my new stuff, and then jumped back in the car to return to Loyola where I'd stay another night and wait for them to take Emma away. Even though she'd been "declared" dead, everything looked as it had before I left. She stayed in the same room. The ventilator continued to fill her lungs with air. Nothing had changed. Nothing but the declaration that my precious little girl wasn't truly there.

Back in the conference room a few more friends had arrived. Cindy, Julie, Denise. Cindy had brought some food. Food? I realized I hadn't eaten in over 24 hours, not since the egg sandwich. The thought of food made me gag; I wanted to throw up. She'd brought soda, too. Diet Pepsi. Okay, that

I could handle. And some honey wheat pretzels. Why I remember those two things when so many other details are fuzzy, I'm not sure. But I do. Perhaps it was because those were the first things I'd eaten since Emma died. Or perhaps because I'd never had those pretzels before. Or maybe it was all the people telling me that I needed to eat, because I had to live. I couldn't quit.

Extended family members continued to show up. One of Bill's aunts from Florida arrived around 7 pm that night. The girls and I had gone to visit her the previous July. Ten days of vacation. It'd been a great trip—one of our favorite. A day at Magic Kingdom in Disney World. Ariel's grotto. Kelsey and Emma getting their picture taken with Ariel. Belle. Cinderella. Such special memories...even in the midst of the extreme heat. The laughter, the fun, the swimming pool. Emma sweetly telling Mickey Goodbye as we left, her head on my shoulder but her hand lifted in a tender wave. Then on to the beach. Hours spent splashing her big sisters. Playing in the waves. Galloping towards the water. Investigating the starfish and sand dollars. Holding up her little dress so it wouldn't get wet, exposing her princess underwear.

Who'd have thought the next time we saw his aunt was because of Emma's death?

She wanted to see Emma one last time. Even though I'd already said Goodbye, even though she'd been declared dead, I took her in. But I didn't like what I saw. The color of her skin. Her tongue. None of it. I wanted to run, far away. And never look back.

Instead, I walked back with her to the conference room.

Plans needed to be made for Emma's visitation... and funeral. I nixed that one right away. I didn't want it called a funeral. That was too depressing, too sad. I wanted a celebration of Emma's life, something happy, joyful. No black. Only Emma's favorite colors—pink, purple...the colors of spring.

But where? I didn't know any funeral homes, had never had any experience with them. Jill spoke up. *What about Conley Funeral Home?* Perfect! I'd worked with Ben, the owner's son, at an ice cream shop years before. I'd heard great things about Bruce, the director, and how he handled funerals with and for kids. She called.

And he came.

That so impressed me. I was still at Loyola. Emma was still in her room, Bill was in his. There was no way I would leave. So Bruce came to me, even though it was late. And we planned what we needed. A casket. Yuck. A vault. Honestly, I didn't even know what that was for. A vault? To lock her up? *No. To keep her safe. No water.* Ah. Yuck. I chose a white coffin, white satin. A cross on the lid. Child-size. A sparkly vault. Yuck.

Bruce wanted to hear about Emma, to get to know her a bit. So I talked. And he listened. I cried. He listened. And then he spoke. Calmed my fear...*was Emma alone in the room when she died?* Emma hated being alone. She never went anywhere in the house by herself. With a family of six I suppose it was kind of hard to get away from everyone. If one of us was upstairs, that's where she'd be. If I left her sleeping and went in the basement to exercise, she'd wake within minutes of my descending and race to find me...crying all the way.

What if she'd been alone in the house and knew it? Did terror fill her little heart; suck the breath from her lungs?

Bruce reminded me of a story from Scripture, a story I'd learned a long time ago but had forgotten. After hearing it again, I felt truth sweep through me with comfort and peace and hope.

The story? A fiery furnace. Shadrach, Meshach and Abednego. Three guys whose story is found in the book of Daniel. Three guys who chose to worship the one true God, and God alone.

Because of their refusal to worship an idol, the king ordered them to be thrown in a fiery furnace—seven times hotter than normal. So hot that the soldiers who threw the men in were instantly killed. Scriptures says best what happened next: "Didn't we tie up three men and throw them into the furnace? 'Yes, your Majesty, we certainly did.' 'Look!' Nebuchadnezzar shouted. 'I see four men, unbound, walking around in the fire unharmed! And the fourth looks like a god." (Daniel 3:24-25)

The men were then called to come out of the furnace. And they did. Unharmed. Scripture says the fire had not touched them; not a hair on their head was singed nor their clothing scorched (Daniel 3:27). And the king praised their God.

And so did I.

Emma was not alone, of that I was sure. I don't understand how but it is not wishful thinking. Bruce believed she was not alone. Scripture convinced me, comforted me. I stood firmly on that truth.

The fire had not touched Emma. Or so I thought. Her hair had not been scorched. I don't know about her nightgown, the purple one with little white stars scattered all over. I never saw it again. But there's a way that God comforts those He loves. There's a certainty that words can't explain. And that's the comfort I received that night while choosing Emma's coffin, after hearing the story of the fiery furnace. She was not alone in the fiery furnace of our home.

Neither was I.

Another story came to mind, truth breathed from Emma's own mouth. Two days before the fire Emma and I drove around town, ran errands. She'd attended a local preschool twice a week. Not always liking it, her preference was to be with me or Bill. Dropping her off had almost always been a struggle.

But that day, strapped safely in her car seat, Emma looked out the van window. Music played; it was a good moment. Emma spoke. *Mommy, I'm not afraid to go to school anymore.* Why not, I asked. *Because I know God is always with me.* Straight from heaven itself through the lips of my little girl. A gift...spoken a mere two days before she died.

Why is it that I'm so quick to offer comfort to others, to remind them of God's love and protection and provision but forget that He offers those same things to me?

I had done that before, forgotten that God's peace is for me, too. It was a few days after Emma had been born. Her bilirubin levels were high—she was jaundiced. Our doctor ordered her to be put under the lights, in a "suitcase" as I affectionately called that contraption. I was a new mom again, full of hormones. My helpless baby with yellow skin. *Keep her eyes covered. She could go blind. Twenty-four hour care.* I was already exhausted, now I needed to watch over Emma. Bill couldn't stay awake that long because of the damage to his brain from the stroke three years before. My mom took the day shift. I had the night. Bad thoughts happen at night.

I prayed for Emma throughout that first night. For safety. For health. For peace. Emma was hungry but we could only feed her in the suitcase. We couldn't hold her, just her hands, her fingers...and tenderly stroke her cheeks.

In the middle of the second night, exhausted, I prayed that Jesus would gently care for her. A picture formed in my mind. Jesus sat in a rocking chair, holding Emma, soothing her. She calmed. Then the picture broadened to show me that His lap was big enough for me, too. In my mind's eye I crawled up and rested and felt peace for the first time since she'd been born.

Was that real? Did I think that really happened? No. But I'm a visual learner. And God knows that, He created me that way. He brings pictures to my mind for comfort. Like that one. And the picture that Emma wasn't alone. Did I experience a vision? I don't think so. But I do know this—I did experience his comfort, his peace that Scripture says passes all understanding (Philippians 4:7). And that was real.

People soon began to leave for that second night. I chose to stay. Cindy had brought an inflatable mattress. Was that allowed in a hospital? They told me not to worry about it. I needed to rest. So I did. After a bit of laughter.

Laughter?

Absolutely. In the midst of the pain God brought very special friends to help me process. There were definitely lots of tears. But I remember lots of giggles, too. Not why we laughed, just that we did. A lot. "A time to cry and a time to laugh. A time to grieve and a time to dance." (Ecclesiastes 3:4) It was many months before I danced but for that moment, laughter worked.

It was going to be a long night, and a sad one. The first time I'd sleep knowing that Emma wasn't alive. Her heart no longer beat. She'd no longer be in that room connected to a bunch of machines set to breathe for her.

I did sleep a bit though, how many minutes or hours, I'm not sure. The mattress Cindy brought helped, made the floor a little more endurable, bearable, sleepable. But it didn't soothe the pain I felt deep in my heart. The crushing, the distance I felt from life. The disconnect and uncertainty. What the heck was going on!? How in the world would I survive?

The next day I woke up...crying. I'd heard a few of my friends as they talked, tried to be quiet. My eyes closed, I pretended to sleep. Pretended the nightmare wasn't real. But I couldn't stay quiet. I couldn't keep the sorrow from escaping into the open. Tears streamed from my eyes, sobs wracked my body. Reality squeezed my heart. Someone came and sat next to me. Silent. Rubbed my back. Took a piece of the pain for me. Made it a little more endurable. Just for that moment. In that second. Maybe I could survive. Only time would tell.

Something else happened during the night... something other than the doctors coming to Emma's room to roll her away, to harvest her organs so others would live. A picture formed in my mind, stuck there. The sight brought me peace and hope and comfort.

A picture of Emma and Jesus. They walked away, hand in hand. Their backs were to me but Emma glanced back over her right shoulder. A tender smile played on her lips. A smile that told me she was okay, she was safe. Lady, our Sheltie who had also died in the fire, jumped around her bare feet along with the rest of our animals, a couple of cats and the hamster Emma had just received for her fifth birthday.

This wasn't a vision nor did I see the exact moment Emma died. But the picture was clear, with distinct colors...vivid. The purple of Emma's nightgown, the black & white of Lady's fur, the white of Jesus' robe, the gold that surrounded them.

A second thought entered my mind. I wanted that picture to be real, needed to touch it. And there was a way for that to happen. A dear friend, Janet, is an incredible artist. As I thought about paintings she'd done before, I realized the colors she used were similar to the ones I pictured in my mind. I wanted to ask her, but how? How do I ask someone to paint a picture of my child who'd just died?

I discussed it with my friends, got their opinions. Would they paint a picture if I asked them? Yes, of course! But would Janet? Call and find out, they counseled; ask, don't assume.

So I did. I called even thought it was still somewhat early....around 10 am. Janet didn't answer. I left a message. How do I remember the time? Because of what happened next. I'd called from the conference room, using my cell. Barely ten minutes later, I walked out, probably towards Bill's room.

There, walking down the hall towards me was Janet. I couldn't believe it. Boy did she drive fast!

Yeah, my brain was a little slow.

We hugged...tight. We cried. This grieving mom leaned on her friend, drew a bit of strength. And then it hit me. I stepped back and asked if she got my message. Her reply? *No, I just felt I needed to come here.*

Another gift of God's goodness.

It was time to ask the question. I explained the picture I'd seen in my mind's eye, described it in as much detail as I could. Would she paint it? *It would be my honor.* More tears but this time tears tinged with joy. One more gift of God's goodness showing me He truly cared about my broken heart.

Then I turned to Cindy, who stood with us. Cindy with her beautiful voice. *And you need to do something, too. You need to write a song about this.* She nodded, said she would.

Sometime during the day the social worker came and explained we had to move out of the conference room. He said that my temporary home could no longer support us. It had to return to its original purpose for meetings, not a hotel room. But it certainly served us well. Safety. Security. The walls absorbed many tears, those initial offerings of sacred sorrow. It had become a bit of hallowed ground those first hours after Emma's death.

Funny how that happens again. Life. It moves on. Once we packed up the stuff—the food, the mattress, the donated clothes—the room looked bare, sterile. No evidence of the sorrow and pain left for its next occupants.

After Emma died, I wanted life to stop. I needed everyone around to acknowledge the magnitude of loss. The devastation that we suffered. The huge hole left in our family, my heart.

That feeling intensified as I walked into the burn ICU for the first time after Emma's body had been removed. The room was still there, just no hint of my little girl remained. An empty bed. Clean white sheets. Machines quiet. Another shock as if ice cold water encompassed my entire body. Then, I looked at Bill, watched as he coughed; fought for life, hacked up black crap...remnants of our home...I fell apart. I don't know if it was Bill's coughing, the emptiness of Emma's hospital room—now waiting for its next patient—or the smell of burned flesh. All I knew was that I couldn't do it anymore. I couldn't move forward. I couldn't face another death.

The lucky recipient of my anguish? Bill's brother, Larry. My war buddy. We'd been through this before on the day of Bill's stroke. Larry and I stood on either side of Bill's bed; my mom at the foot. We'd just been told that Bill had suffered a minor stroke at home. But he was talking again. And we were talking with him. Larry on one side, me on the other. It was in the middle of a sentence that it happened, the rest of the stroke. Bill just kind of disappeared. He didn't collapse or shake; the seizure came later. He just kind of stopped, sank back into the bed, disappeared.

We looked at Bill, looked at each other. We watched as the nurse flicked the needle to administer the medication. What in the world happened? We'd just discussed the treatment—TPA, a super-clot buster that'd been used with heart patients but was new for stroke victims. Bill would be the fourth person in the county to receive it for a stroke. Timing was everything. The results were unknown. One person had died; one stayed the same; and one experienced about eighty percent recovery.

Which would happen to Bill?

Larry and his wife, Kate, walked through that experience with me. And then later, after his recovery, with Bill. But it felt like war buddies with Larry. We both saw the same thing. He stayed with me, watched out for me, waited as we heard Bill's prognosis. *Either death or a vegetable.* Less than three months after we'd been married.

And here we were again. Facing death...together. Watched as Bill suffered...again. I cried. Larry comforted. He didn't try to fix it, or even really calm me down. He just let me be...sad...distraught. No expectations. No instructions. Simply a strong shoulder to cry on.

I have no idea how I would've survived without the support of my family and friends. My parents watched over Kelsey. Dana and Matt had their mom. Larry and Kate, my brother, Kevin, Bonnie, Jill, and Cindy watched out for me. They made sure I ate, slept...even shopped.

Yes, shopping again. Because in the midst of Emma's death, and Bill's struggle to live, reality still set in. We'd lost everything; we had nothing. My parents took Kelsey to get clothes, my sister-in-law, Dawn, took Dana. Matt still had most of his stuff because he lived with his mom at the time. Cindy and Jill took me. And what an experience that turned out to be!

There was a mall a little ways from the hospital. I had an idea what I needed to get—basically everything: shoes, pants, shirts, even a coat. We headed to one of my favorite stores and in a matter of minutes—about twenty to be exact—I had replaced some of my clothes. $800 worth. This shocked Jill, which was kind of fun, given the circumstances.

But it was hard walking through the mall. I was so grateful not to be alone. My trip to the store the day before hadn't gone so well. How would I react when I saw kids around Emma's age? Or heard them crying? Would I be jealous or angry? Would I burst out in tears?

We left the first store in search of another. As we walked, Cindy on one side and Jill on the other, a question floated to the surface. I love perfume. I thought about getting some to replace what I had. But in that moment, in light of all that'd happened, it felt like an extravagance, unnecessary. How could I want something like perfume when Emma had died and Bill fought for his life? It wasn't that we couldn't afford it. Bonnie had been in touch with the insurance company. Money was deposited in our account, enough for us to live for a while, to replace some of the things we needed.

Perfume was hardly a necessity. I decided to ask what my friends though. *Did you have perfume before?* They asked. *Yes.* I replied, and then realized what they meant. Permission granted. It was okay to purchase perfume, something extra, even in the midst of what had happened, what we'd lost.

On we shopped. This time in search of the perfect perfume. Not something I'd worn before but something that would remind me of Emma. That would keep my focus on the truth of where she was, in heaven, rather than on the pain of life without her.

At the perfume counter I saw a box of items I liked. Eternity. The exact reminder that I needed! Five items were inside. Even better...more. The box wasn't marked with a price so I asked. Shock zapped me as the lady took the box from me and showed me a different one, one with two items. She said it was a better deal. Now while I'm not the best at math, I did know that five is more than two. At that moment I wanted the set with five. All I needed was the price, not a better deal.

She didn't get it.

So I told her no thanks and kept looking. And guess what I found? Another box, the one with five items, listed at the same price as the one the lady tried to sell with only two. My mistake....I showed it to her and said I wanted to purchase it. She took the box from me...again...and proceeded to tell me that the box had been mismarked. I couldn't have it. Not even at a different price.

Alright. My dad's been a salesman, a VP. He taught me better. The customer's always right. It wasn't my fault they'd mismarked the box. And then she tried to sell me the box with two...again. Wow. Somehow the idea that I wanted the one with more didn't settle in. So in true Turner fashion, I said *never mind* and stormed away, ticked. Jill didn't know what to say. Cindy wasn't there.... she'd been scoping out the shoes.

As Jill and I walked, anger boiled inside. *This lady needed to know what she just did.* Uh, oh. I turned around, fuming, yet calm...if that's even possible. I stepped up to the counter, Jill a step behind. I interrupted the lady's conversation with another sales clerk. *Excuse me.* I said. *I need you to know something.* And then I let her have it. Said it all. All I wanted to do was buy some perfume and she wouldn't let me. I wanted to experience a moment of happiness in my otherwise crappy day. I told her that, too. I explained that she needed to realize she had an opportunity to make someone happy, to make a difference. There was no way to know what was happening in someone's life as they walk up to the counter. But she could help, bring a smile. All I wanted was the box of perfume I'd shown her. But she kept it from me. And it was a bad day, a really bad day. My house burned down. I had nothing. My daughter just died and my husband was still in the hospital. At that point I didn't know if he'd live or die. All I wanted was the perfume and felt she needed to know how she made an already horrible day worse.

Then I walked away.

I refused to listen to her response, didn't want to hear it. Jill tried to keep up. I walked quickly, looked down at the floor when it hit me. *She just got the brunt of my anger from all this, didn't she?* Jill simply looked at me. Great. Now what? And to top it off, I didn't even get the perfume.

My wise friend asked me if I still wanted it, the perfume. I did, but not from that store. Not from that lady. Jill told me she'd go back and get it, without me.

Good. I still needed some shoes for Emma's services.

Jill walked back to the lion's den while Cindy and I searched for shoes. I tried them on and made a few decisions, a couple of purchases. Jill still hadn't returned. Cindy heard what had happened and felt bad for Jill. What took her so long? Was she getting reamed for my behavior? Cindy and I sat down, waited. I wondered if we should go find her. We stood up to head towards the perfume counter. Then we saw her, walking towards us.

With two large shopping bags...one in each hand.
My first thought? *What'd she buy with my money? I only wanted a box...not the store!* Her first

words? *You made out like a bandit!* Jill explained how she told the original sales lady that all I'd said was true...my daughter died in a house fire...yesterday...my husband was still in the hospital...and we really didn't have anything but the clothes on our backs.

The lady tried to cover her mistake until the other two heard what she'd done, how I felt, what had happened. They moved her out of the way, sold Jill the desired box at the original price and proceeded to fill two other bags with every possible gift of perfume they had to give away. I was set.

Through it I learned an important lesson. I make so many assumptions in life; we all do. We don't realize what might be happening in someone else's life. Whether we're in line at the store, the gas station or waiting for the light to change, we have an opportunity to make someone's day better or worse. There's no way to know if they're coming from the dentist, the doctor, or a grave. Life isn't really about us, not as much as we think. Everyone comes in with their own stuff. And we need to remember that.

Chapter 7
The House

"Every act of creation is first an act of destruction."
Pablo Picasso

It was time to go home, to see my house. I had to set eyes on the destruction, the devastation, to figure out what was left.

I packed up my new clothes, said bye to Bonnie who stayed behind to watch over things at the hospital, and headed back to my mom and dad's. Once at their house, I took another shower to finally rid the stench of smoke from my hair.

Then, I asked my mom to drive me to my house, so I could get my car and see the damage. When we arrived one of Bill's cousins was there with his wife. They stayed while I took in the ruined remains. I was shocked at what I saw. Sheets of plywood enclosed every window. From the front it didn't look too bad. A sign was posted on our garage. *Condemned.* A sign in our grass. *Gunderson Family Fund. For donations and update go to:* www.thewindings.org *or* www.ccclife.org. I walked to the south side of the house, the worst part. Plywood covered every square inch. My blue house was now tan, the color of the plywood. The back of the house was covered, too.

The front door stood open. The new front door. I had no idea what happened to our original doors. If the firemen took them off, destroyed them, what had happened. I had to go inside. No, I wasn't supposed to go in, but I had to. I needed to see what was left, how bad it really was...to grasp the cause of Emma's death, Bill's injuries.

Nothing prepared me for what I was to experience.

The acrid smell assaulted my senses first. The smell of a burned life, years of memories, hopes and dreams. And the darkness. Not a single window left open on the first floor. The only light shone through the open door. I stepped inside to my past. It was barely recognizable. The ceiling seemed lower, perhaps because of the amount of debris on the floor. The ash and soot. Bill's office, the first room to the left, now opened into the family room, the wall disintegrated between the two rooms. Or rather, what was left of the family room.

I looked at the remains of Bill's desk, that beautiful mahogany piece of art. Dark soot blanketed everything. Emma's play riding horse lay on its side, leg missing, eyes staring. The computer monitor sat on the desk, partially melted. The walls stained with smoke and water, an ugly pattern of swirls and stripes and nothingness.

The stairs leading to the second story stood before me, beckoned. Would I ascend them? No. Not that day. Not only because it wasn't safe, but because I wasn't ready to see the place where Emma had drawn her final breath.

I walked down the hallway to the kitchen. Everything was gone: our kitchen table, the cabinets, the walls. Even the refrigerator was simply a melted piece of sheet metal. The only reason I recognized it because of its location in the room. The island disintegrated into the floor, the only hint of the dishwasher was a small square of wire, a few broken dishes still stacked inside. I could see into the bathroom, one of Emma's favorite places to play, from where I stood. Through the wall, behind the stove, or what was left of it.

To the left of the kitchen used to be our family room. The place where our family played and spent time together. The place that held our laughter and memories, our Christmas trees and toys. Absolutely nothing left. Just the brick of the fire place. No pictures. No TV. No couch or chairs. All was gone, including the ceiling.

I'd heard from Tony, the Good Samaritan, that right before he slipped on that patch of ice, he'd gone around the back of the house to see what was happening inside. He glanced through the sliding glass door in the kitchen as the family room ceiling collapsed into the burning inferno. A short fifteen minutes after the fire had started.

I looked up and saw our bed. The rest of our bedroom was gone, burned up in flames, smothered in smoke. The yellow tip of Emma's blanket hung limply over the side.

Bill's cousin and I searched some more. I picked around the dining room, scavenging any piece of the past I could salvage, any memory I could hold. Until finally…I was done. I'd had enough. The smell overwhelmed me. The remains of our burned life were too much to bear. I had to leave…quickly… and, as I walked out the front door, I took pieces of our house with me…stuck to the bottom of my new shoes.

Outside in the yard, parts of my dresser lay on its side exposed for the entire world to see, including some of my clothes. Reality hit once again. Things lost. My jewelry. My grandmothers' rings—one from each grandma. Gone. Heirlooms. Would the pain never end?

I told Bill's cousin about my desire to visit the Elburn Fire Department. I'd heard through a few people that the firemen struggled with Emma's death. I had a picture of her and my niece, Linsey I wanted to share so they could see Emma as I remembered her. Alive. Smiling. A protective and loving arm around her little cousin. He asked if I wanted them to go with me. I said yes.

We drove down Route 47. I clocked how long it took, wondered how fast the fire trucks drove just a couple days before. About six minutes doing the speed limit. I still wondered why it felt like it'd been so long for them to get there. The Elburn Fire Chief, Kelly Callahan, told me it'd taken them twelve minutes from the time they received the call to the time they arrived at my house. Not soon enough, but not their fault.

I drove into the parking lot of the station...and sat. Anxiety filled my heart. How would I react? What would I say? I had no idea. I just wanted to offer a bit of comfort and a reminder that they did their job. It wasn't their fault Emma hadn't lived. It was part of God's plan—the number of her days had already been determined. (Psalm 139:16) I didn't like it, but that wasn't the point. The point was that I had an opportunity to reach out and encourage those in need, those who had risked their lives for my little girl. It was the least I could do.

Walking up to the building alone, I knocked on the door. A fireman named Matt answered. I explained who I was. Matt replied he'd been at my house, a burned ear from my super-heated house fire. I cried as I thanked him and showed him the picture of the child he risked his life to save. I gave a piece of Emma away when I handed that picture to him, to put up in the station where it still hangs for them to remember. Not of failure, but of life. They need to remember to give their best and work their hardest because that's all that's expected. The rest really isn't up to us.

Chapter 8
Celebrating Emma

"Celebrate what you want to see more of." Thomas J. Peters

Friday night arrived, and with it plans began to unfold: where we'd stay that weekend, what we'd do. I started to look towards another day, beyond the next moment for the first time since I caught that glimpse of smoke swirling from our home. The plan...how to celebrate Emma's life.

I'd spoken with Bruce from the funeral home about the details of Emma's casket and vault, but none of the other plans had been finalized: the dates and times, the details of the celebration. Apparently, Conley's Funeral Home was too small. As the word of Emma's death spread, Christ Community received call after call from concerned people both within the church and within the community. They sought the details—where would the visitation be? The service? What time? What day?

I'm not a detail person.

But decisions had to be made, right down to each song, each picture, and each person who would share. Asking someone to speak at your child's celebration service, no matter how joyful I tried to make the event, was difficult. Knowing who I wanted was easy, actually saying the words, not so much. I asked one man from each side of my family—Bill's brother, Larry, and my brother, Kevin—to share thoughts about Emma, stories of her laughter and love. Neither brother, Larry nor Kevin, hesitated to say yes. Emma loved both of her uncles so much. My boss, Larry, would greet and share about the impact of the community...how people reached out to us from our subdivision, the church, and many that we didn't even know. Jim, our senior pastor, would help keep our eyes fixed on the bigger picture; he would give the message, share a word from Scripture.

Part of the community's response, I think, came because of our history in St. Charles. I grew up there, went through the school system. My brother, my parents...and even me...we've all had influence within the Fox Valley area. Word spread and people wanted to respond, to share the pain as best they could through cards, generous donations and provision for our family to help replace all that was lost.

Replace all...except Emma.

I kept focused on the purpose of the nights: to celebrate her life. Although she's lost to us here on earth, I know I will see her again. I trust that she'll be waiting for me when it's my turn to go home...to heaven. Until then, the party must go on, to share the joy of her life, the impact she had on so many. And we'd need room to serve all who wanted to be there with us. Emma's visitation and celebration was held at Christ Community, the place she said she loved the most, next to our home. It only seemed right.

Ron, one of the pastors at church, came to Loyola so we could determine those details of her services. We chose the dates and times so people would be available to attend. Except Bill, he wouldn't be there. He was still in a coma. While he'd miss her service, I'd decided to wait for the burial; to allow Bill to see her one last time...if he lived.

There was another part in planning her celebration that I had to think of...what she would wear, her final outfit. I knew what I wanted.

My mom had recently celebrated her 60th birthday. Her birthday wish was to take all the "Turner girls" for a day at the American Girl Place in downtown Chicago. At first the plan was to go in January, just after her and Emma's birthdays which were only a day apart, something special to them both. Unfortunately, there was a lot of snow that winter, so much so that we couldn't head down-town as planned. Mom rescheduled for February, four days before the fire.

The Saturday before the beast destroyed our home, the Turner girls...my mom, sister-in-law, Dawn, niece Linsey, Dana, Kelsey, Emma and I... drove down to the city together. The day was per-fect. Lunch and shopping, shopping and lunch... what more could we girls want? Emma was par-ticularly excited to see all the dolls and toys. On the way home she described how she felt about the trip...*that was the bestest day of my whole life!* Little did we know.

While Emma looked at the dolls with Kelsey, I saw the dress I wanted to purchase for her to wear at Easter. It was beautiful and in her favorite color: purple. Flowers graced the bottom. There was even a matching dress for her new baby doll. I managed to sneak them home that day with-out Emma knowing. Unfortunately, the dress lay crumbled, unusable, still in the shopping bag as firemen plowed through our house to fighting the flames that consumed our home.

My sister-in-law, Kate, got a replacement dress for me. A detail I didn't need to worry about, a pre-cious offering of help. She purchased one and passed it along to Conley's. Dawn, my other sister-in-law, took care of Emma's shoes and tights. White patent leather shoes.

Honestly, I wondered why Emma needed shoes. It wasn't like she'd walk again. And really, she hated to wear them. As soon as she'd walk in the door, or often while still sitting in the van, she'd kick off her shoes and wiggle those little toes, freeing them as she scampered about the house.

Another decision made...I wanted to speak, needed to. So many were worried about my state of mind, how I was handling Emma's death. It was important to let them see I was okay. That God was in control. I felt a deep desire to share, to speak, to honor not only my daughter, but my Savior.

But I was scared.

———————

JOURNAL ENTRY
March 8, 2005
Day Six
Dear Lord, I feel like my heart has been ripped to shreds. Emma is dead. To us, anyway. You have her now.

I praise you because you are in control. I praise you because you are love. I praise you because you weep with me.

And now, as I face the celebration of her life, I pray you would give me strength. I pray you would give me courage. I pray you would give me your words so that the truth of your love would reign supreme. Help me to be real. Help me to be transparent. Help me to cry and laugh. Use my feeble words to show how great and awesome you are!

All weekend I tried to focus on what I would say. How in the world would I tell a bunch of people about the impact my little girl had on my life? How much I breathed with her, loved her, and would now hurt without her? How could I summarize five years of her life, the memories, to provide a glimpse into the incredible gift Emma was to our family? Overwhelmed, I stopped thinking, decided to put it off, not think about those questions for just for a couple of days. We desperately needed a distraction, some time away from the intensity of our feelings and the circumstances we faced, the thoughts, the fears. So I chose to head to a hotel with the girls. Not that I didn't want to stay with my mom and dad. I did. I just needed some space to process, to breathe.

But I also didn't want to be completely alone. Cindy stayed with us the first night and Jill stayed the second. Dana, Kelsey and I were never by ourselves those beginning days without Emma. Someone watched over us, sat with us. And even shopped with us.

Yes, shopping again.

The three of us needed clothes. We had to find something to wear for the visitation and celebration. But what do you wear to your child's services? How do you worry about what you look like when all that is in front of you is your daughter's body... still...silent...unmoving?

But we had to find something nice. So we shopped with Cindy. A great distraction for such a dismal task. It took while...especially with three girls in search of clothes. But we met our task, found suitable clothes. Ones we'd never wear again. Too many memories.

Those moments at the hotel and the time shopping served as a great diversion against what was to come. My thoughts kept returning to services, about what I would say, who would show up, how it'd all go. One specific thought fixated in my mind, one particular event, one moment to come...the first time I'd see Emma's body.

I dreaded that moment. Dreamed of it, actually. Really didn't want it to happen. But no amount of wishing or hoping could stop time from ticking forward, forcing me closer to that horrendous second when my eyes would focus on that tiny casket. What would I do? How would I react? I hadn't seen many dead bodies before. This time it was my own daughter's body that would lie there life-less...no more air flowing through her lungs, no longer breathing.

Time passed and our brief weekend retreat ended. The girls and I returned to my parents' house. Reality summoned us once more. The day of the visitation had arrived. After putting on our new clothes, we headed off to church. I hadn't been there since the day before the fire. How drastically different my life had become.

Fortunately, my dad decided to drive us. It was late afternoon, the sun not yet set. He drove up the long driveway and as he stopped in front of the church, I saw it. The sign. *Celebrating the Life of Emma Jo.*

I sobbed. Tears poured. Yes, it's a celebration. But it's also the end. This was it. In that moment all I could do what focus on my breathing. Nothing else mattered...breathe in, and then out. In...out. I stepped out of the car and we walked inside. Bruce waited for us. He led us to a waiting room. My heart raced. My breath quickened. Soon it would be time to see Emma, her body.

Family members began to arrive. The waiting room filled with people who knew Emma, missed Emma, who loved her. Bruce took a few minutes to explain what we'd see, how the night would transpire. They'd created a line in the atrium. A purple and pink balloon arch greeted every visitor. Pictures boards displayed glimpses of memories, lovingly created by my mom, my cousin, Kelly, and our neighbor, Becky. Snapshots of Emma's life. *Click*. But there was not a single picture from our house, taken with my camera, when Emma looked at me as I caught a memory forever freezing it in time.

But I did have one thing, her favorite toy. A pink unicorn she'd made herself. Somehow it'd been saved along with a couple other stuffed animals. I thought they'd been in the house, ruined by the water and soot and smoke. But over the weekend, I'd remembered where they were, left in the van inside the garage...untouched. A gift of God's goodness. That unicorn was something we held knowing that she'd held it in her arms, too. A squeeze of the unicorn was now the closest thing I had to squeezing Emma.

Bruce talked with the kids, described what they'd see, what Emma's body would look like in the casket. He explained what death was like...that she'd look like she was sleeping but she wasn't really there. While the part we loved and touched was still visible, the part that made Emma...*Emma*... was gone...with her Savior.

Then came the dreadful moment: Bruce asked if I was ready to see Emma, gently inquired if I wanted someone to accompany me. I chose to go alone. The walk through the atrium felt like an eternity, as if the room would never end. Sensitive, Bruce encouraged me to take my time, said there was no rush.

I walked into the Welcome Center, the room where they'd set Emma's coffin. I hadn't wanted any flowers. Instead I requested that donations be made in Emma's memory to our building campaign... the one for a new children's ministry space that had just begun. As I walked into the room, I saw some flowers. Drapes covered with Disney princesses and My Little Ponies, two of her favorite things, blocked my initial view of the casket.

Tears started to flow. My breathing quickened as my heart raced...and then stopped...all at the same time. Once again my focus shifted to the air that flowed in and out of my lungs, one breath at a time, the only reality I could count on at the moment. I rounded the makeshift screen and there it stood.

The casket.

With Emma's body inside.

Feelings and fear flowed through the core of my being, threatened to implode. My hands shook with sorrow. Surely this was the moment I dreaded. The one of complete release, total devastation; the moment everyone'd been waiting to happen. I was about to die right beside her.

I fell to my knees before the tiny child-size casket. Emma lay there in her purple dress, a white shirt underneath. Apparently there'd been a burn on her body after all. But I never saw it. At this moment all I saw was my baby. My precious girl. My complete despair.

Sobs wracked my body. I touched her hair. Waited for her to smile, to giggle, to sit up and try to startle me...say it was all a cruel joke. Instead I looked at her tender skin, no longer soft to the touch. Her eyes closed, no longer able to stare into mine. A tiny smile fixed on her face, as if she knew something more than I did.

And just before that moment came, the one that threatened complete collapse, something happened. A precious gift of hope. A conversation entered my mind. Not the kind of actual voices, more like thoughts...Emma's thoughts.

Why is my mommy crying? Doesn't she know I'm with you?

Eleven simple words. A truth and then peace completely flooded my soul. An assurance that Emma was okay. That she was in the presence of Jesus himself. An almost holy moment that brought strength and power and comfort.

Yes, I knew Emma was with Jesus. I knew that she was safe; she wasn't hurt or scared or lonely. Jesus told us that He was preparing a place for each one of us. "Don't let your hearts be troubled. Trust in God, and trust also in me. There is more than enough room in my Father's home. If this were not so, would I have told you that I am going to prepare a place for you? When everything is ready, I will come and get you, so that you will always be with me where I am. And you know the way to where I am going." (John 14:1-3)

Heaven became reality in that moment. Yes, I'd known it existed, believed what the Bible said. But right now, it *felt* real. A breath whispered through my soul, made me yearn for it and filled me with comfort.

Comfort and strength enough to stand for over six hours as person after person walked through the line to see Emma, to console my family, to support us. Six hours, over 900 people. I knew we were loved but the sheer number overwhelmed me. And yet I felt great assurance from the number. Each person who walked through that line took a piece of the pain; shared in my sorrow; gave me strength to keep going.

My family was there; not just my parents and brother and his family or Bill's family. My extended family: family from Ohio, New Jersey and Pennsylvania. My grandmother, my mom's mom. A mom who'd lost a daughter over sixty years before I lost Emma. When my mom told Gram was coming, I was shocked. She didn't travel anymore; not since the accident where she'd lost her leg. It was too hard, traveling with a wheelchair. But Gram made the trek with my cousins and their parents across country in a van. For me. For Emma. Because of her love for us.

There were so many others. Many I knew. My fifth grade teacher. Friends from church. Teachers from Emma's preschool. And lots of people I didn't know. Neighbors. Friends and co-workers of the rest of my family. And kids. Lots of kids from our children's ministry. Kids who were Emma's own age. Who had to glimpse death for the first time at such a tender age.

I didn't stand there alone. My close friends were there. Bonnie. Cindy. Jill. My cousin, Kelly. They never left my side. Made sure I ate, drank water, and sat when I needed to...even though I didn't. Kelsey stood nearby, too. Holding Emma's unicorn. I didn't want to put it in the casket. I needed to keep it; hold it when I felt sad...tried to catch a scent of Emma's breath, her skin, a memory.

Every once in a while my brother would walk through the line, startling me. He took it upon himself to keep me posted on the length of time it took from the end of the line to get to me, the family, to Emma. A moment of humor.

How can I ever say thank you to so many people who helped me and my family endure the pain of Emma's death? Words aren't enough. I was overwhelmed. But I trust they know. Those who were there, those who cared.

The care didn't stop with the visitation. Mail started arriving at my parents' house. Card after card, often with gift cards or checks inside. People I knew. So many more I didn't. *You don't know me but...*I lost track of how many people signed their cards that way. In the end we received cards from almost every state in the country, as well as a couple from other countries. Where there weren't cards, there were emails full of words of encouragement and sympathy. Those words brought comfort and compassion, they filled part of the hole in my heart, allowed me to put one foot in front of the other and endure.

Some told me that night at the visitation that I wouldn't remember much about it. That the people and lines and words would all blur together.

They haven't.

I remember. Because I need to. In those moments when collapse threatens, words of solace and faces come back to me; remind me of God's grace and love shown through the tears of those who were there. The hugs. The whispers of sorrow.

I remember.

I remember one family. Bonnie's sister, her husband and their kids. The kids had been in our children's ministry when they were younger. The oldest told Bonnie he didn't want to follow a God who could do this to a family, to me. He gave his Bible to her, didn't want it anymore.

His face is clear in my mind as I remember how he stood before me. Eye to eye. *Please don't let this get between you and God.* I told him. *I'm okay.* Because in that moment, I was okay. And in the bigger picture, I am okay. But to think someone might turn his back on God because of an event in my life...not if I could help it.

Another family comes to mind. A little girl with the same name and age as my little girl. Our two Emma's—one, mine...Emma Jo. The other...Emma Joy. A precious girl whom now offers my "Emma hugs".

Co-workers. Friends. Friends of family. Strangers. Paramedics. Firemen. Those who were at my house that day. I hugged them tight; introduced them to my little girl. Wished they could've known her when she was alive.

A tender and very personal, ceremony ended that first night as we remembered Emma. Tucking in, Bruce called it. The final goodbye. A literal time where I tucked Emma's body in, pulled a covering over her body as if she were going to sleep, instead of being buried.

Bruce asked our family to come forward, to stand around Emma's casket. One by one, our final goodbyes were uttered, our last farewell given. Tears streamed. Words of love whispered. As I touched Emma's tender face, her cute little nose, ran my fingers through the ends of her hair, a piece of my heart tumbled into that casket. A piece that I doubt will ever return. Then I took the satin sheet that lay at her feet and gently tucked my little girl in one final time.

And my heart shattered. Again.

JOURNAL ENTRY
March 9, 2005
Day Seven

Father in heaven, I miss my Emma. My heart is breaking and yet I'm feeling totally numb. I can't believe Emma died. I can't believe a fire destroyed my house. I don't think I'm in denial—I think I'm in disbelief. This just can't be true.

And yet I know it is. Emma is gone from me. And I am so sad. I am amazed at how people have told me how much harder it's going to get—as if I won't know. As if I didn't realize the extent of my love for Emma.

But, oh Jesus, I want to love you more. I want to be willing to carry this cross—this burden—so that you may be glorified and honored. Help me to proclaim your name. Help me to talk to others about you.

Please give Emma a kiss for me. And tell her that I love her and miss her so terribly much.

———

The celebration service was the next night, in the main auditorium at Christ Community Church. There wasn't even a question if that was an okay room to use—if it might be too large. It wasn't. Any other room in the building would've been too small.

Once again we sat in the waiting room, waited for the service to begin. Waited for people to arrive. Waited to stand before them, to share about Emma.

I'd asked two of my friends to sing—Cindy and Chris, one of the guys with whom I worked with in children's ministry. Cindy sang "I Can Only Imagine" by Mercy Me, a song depicting what might happen the moment we stood before Jesus in heaven. Would we dance? Or be silent. I liked to picture Emma dancing, skipping, even running with excitement and pure joy. Chris sang, "Untitled Hymn" by Chris Rice. Another picture of a life, from birth to death and everything in between. A call to a life following Jesus, ending with a gentle reminder...to fly to Him, to be in his presence. I love the words of that song despite my heart's desire to have Emma with me.

People arrived and it was time for our family to head in. We walked to the front of the auditorium, and sat in the front row, Emma's casket in before us. My boss, Larry, welcomed everyone to the celebration. He shared about the response of the community, the support and care our family received. Not just me. My parents. My brother and his family. Bill's brother and his family. My kids. Even our church family.

Larry, Bill's brother, spoke representing the Gunderson family. Kevin, for the Turners. Then it was our turn, my family. Matt, Dana, Kelsey and I all chose to share memories of Emma, precious gifts of memories for others to catch a glimpse of life in our family. Perfect snapshots of each. Matt imploring the family to make amends and move forward together. Dana, forgetful, dashed from the stage in what looked like extreme sorrow when, in reality, she couldn't find the paper with her notes written out. Kelsey, my first-born turned middle then youngest but somehow the oldest, shared tender memories of why she was Emma's *bestest sister* ever.

And then came my turn.

What do you say at the celebration of your daughter's life? How can one convey the intensity of love, the years of living, the tender gift she'd been—and continues to be—in my life? I'd tried preparing earlier that day. I wanted to write it out. But every time I started, words didn't seem like enough. I finally sensed to be still, to trust once again. To be silent so I could sense the words God wanted me to speak.

So the world may know.

For the sake of the neighbors.

To use our story to tell others about Christ. People would listen. I knew they would. Use it.

Shared spotlights of Emma's love, packed in five short years of life. It so often overwhelmed me. Now I know. She had to—so I could continue to live on without her.

Songs were sung. Pictures shown. A song—"A Girl Like Me"—Kelsey, Emma and I used to sing together in the van now played to snapshots of Emma with friends and family. And then came "Jesus Loves Me". Pictures of Emma alone in hopes of giving a glimpse of her spirit, her humor, her love, her energy.

Finally, the message from our Senior Pastor, Jim. Another gift of peace, of truth. "When you pass through the waters, I will be with you; and when you pass through the rivers, they will not sweep over you. When you walk through the fire, you will not be burned; the flames will not set you ablaze." (Isaiah 43:2 NIV)

Yes, trials come. Things are hard...really hard. But God's Word promises that we won't be completely consumed. And we're not. Even in the midst of suffering. Even when a child dies. The truth doesn't take away the pain, but it does provide purpose, perseverance, the ability to keep on keeping on. Until the day comes when I'll breathe my last, and finally stand and dance before my Savior, knowing Emma will dance right beside me.

Chapter 9
Telling Bill

"Can you hold His hand and let everything else go?" Charles Spurgeon

Life slowed down a bit after Emma's services ended and families returned home. I hadn't yet returned to work, but still had a lot to do. The house stood burned, vacant. Bill's health...and life...was still uncertain. A new normal soon took control.

JOURNAL ENTRY
March 12, 2005

Day ten—I can't believe I've been without Emma for ten days. Am I still in shock? I really don't know.

It's all so surreal.

And Bill—he's not really any better nor any worse. His burns are healing but his lungs are not. Pneumonia has taken over. I really don't know how to pray. Would his heart survive without Emma? Could I survive without him?

Lord God, you know my heart's desire. I want a husband who loves me and cares for me. A man who protects me and cherishes me. I don't think I can handle having a shell for a husband. But I desire to obey you even more. I choose to follow you. I am so grateful that you are walking with me through this darkest time of my life.

I need you.

I need you to sustain me, to comfort me. I need your wisdom and your guidance. Help me to stand firm. Please don't let me stray. Keep my feet planted firmly on your rock. Be my shield, my protector. Be the lover of my soul.

Please give me your peace that passes all understanding. Give Emma a special squeeze for me. I miss her so much. Help me to know she is safe with you.

JOURNAL ENTRY
March 20, 2005

Day eighteen of an entirely new life. I think I'm still processing the fact that I no longer have Emma. The reality is slowly setting in but I know I still have a long way to go.

I miss you, Emma.

But on to good news—Bill is breathing on his own. He's off medication. His pneumonia is gone. The doctors are slowly waking him up. Larry and I even communicated a bit with him today.

He, too, has a long road of recovery ahead of him. Rehab for his body and counseling for his heart.

Lord, I have no idea how this is all going to play out. I'm nervous and scared to tell Bill that Emma died.

That's still so weird to say—Emma died. She is no longer alive. My little Emma.

Sometimes my heart goes down the path towards asking why. Then I think of your words that tell me how much higher your ways are than my ways and your thoughts compared to my thoughts (Isaiah 55:8-9).

It's not that I can't be sad and mourn Emma's death. I am just trusting that you have a far bigger plan in this than I could ever imagine.

"Faith is being sure of what we hope for and certain of what we do not see." (Hebrews 11:1 NIV)

That is now my verse. Lord, I want to be sure of heaven. I want to be sure of Emma being with you right now. I want to be sure that you have a big-

ger plan in all this—much bigger than I could ever imagine. I want to be certain because right now, I can't see it. I can't even see what will happen tomorrow.

But I trust you.

Please give Emma a squeeze for me.

It was time to tell Bill about Emma. One of the worst moments that followed her death. I had to tell him that Emma had died, in a house fire. One he might not remember. Three weeks before.

I dreaded that day. March 22, 2005. Two days before my birthday. Services were over. People returned to their lives. But I couldn't return to mine... not like before. This was new. Unchartered. And once again, fear consumed me.

How would he respond? What would he say? I feared his reaction...would he give up or fight to survive or simply quit life? Become a shell of a man, alive on the outside but completely dead inside? I needed him to understand, to catch up. I couldn't mourn Emma alone, without my husband. Uncertainty filled me.

This was Emma. His baby girl. And I had to tell him that she'd died. Bill loved each of his kids but he and Emma had a special bond. They spent so much time together, every Wednesday when I was at work. They played with her ponies, dug in the dirt, mowed the grass, and fed the ducks at the river, explored every inch of the land we owned. How in the world would he respond when he heard that she was gone?

I held conversations in my mind, tried to anticipate it all so I'd be prepared to cry, to comfort, to stand and breathe.

The doctors started waking Bill up on Monday. I would tell him on Tuesday. I believed I had to do this alone. I'm his wife. Emma was ours. A family member wanted to be there when I told him. In fact, she was quite upset when she'd found out I'd told him without her. Really? She wasn't there when Emma was conceived, or even born, so why would she think it'd be appropriate to be there when I told Emma's daddy that she'd died?

My focus returned to my husband.

JOURNAL ENTRY
Day Nineteen
March 21, 2005

Bill is waking up more and more. At this point it looks like I will be telling him about Emma tomorrow. Larry told me that the doctor would like to see him sitting up and possibly moving and walking.

Oh Abba, I don't know how to tell my husband that our daughter died almost three weeks ago.

I feel sick to my stomach.

I've already gone through the wake and celebration—I didn't think I could make it through that.

Now I'm not sure how I'll make it through telling Bill.

Lord God, you are in control. I trust your faithfulness. I trust your plan. It certainly doesn't mean I'm not hurting, because I am. I'm just choosing to trust you.

It's still so difficult to believe that this isn't all a dream—a nightmare. I wish it was and that I'd wake up soon. Then I'd have Emma again.

Jesus, please go before me. Please prepare Bill's heart for this news. Don't let him give up. Don't let him quit. I need my husband—and I need him whole.

Give me the right words to say. Please don't let this become a wall between us. I pray we are drawn closer together and closer to you.

But oh how my hearts aches in pain. Actually, it hurts so much that I'm numb. As I think of Emma,

*there are stabs that go deep. But it still hasn't hap-
pened.*

*Bless us with sleep tonight. Comfort my family—
those who loved Emma.*

And don't let us forget.

Goodnight, sweet Emma. I love you!

———

Because Bill was waking up and the realization
came that he might not have any clue what had
happened, I asked people to wait to visit Bill until
after he knew about Emma. I needed to know if
he wanted to see anyone. If together, we could
handle visitors. Bill loved being around people,
especially his family, but when he hurts, like a lot
of people, he retreats to heal. He'd need a lot of
healing after this tragedy.

But I needed someone there with me, to support
me as I shared this news with Emma's daddy. Bonnie and Kate stayed in the waiting area. They stood
by as I gave the worst news I could possibly share
with my husband. Matt showed up later, was our
comic relief.

The first time I said the words, *Emma died*, my heart
raced. Bill had a tracheotomy because of his lung
injury and low oxygen levels. He couldn't talk,
couldn't convey what he thought. Once again I

had to anticipate what he was thinking, what he wanted to know...just like after his stroke.

I explained there'd been a fire...his eyes got wide. That he'd been hurt...they grew wider. The house destroyed. He shook his head. And then the despicable words...*Emma died in the fire.* Bill's response? Nothing.

Great.

He didn't get it.

I tried again. *There was a fire. It happened a few weeks ago. You were hurt. Emma was home with you. But she died. She didn't make it.* Bill nodded his head. Mouthed *huh, that's too bad.*

This wasn't going the way I'd planned. Or hoped. With the extent of the trauma and the effects from a three-week coma, his brain was still a little fuzzy. Or perhaps it was God's grace, gently allowing Bill to process those weeks of life in a matter of minutes, to absorb the truth of what had occurred.

He kept gesturing to his legs, curious why they were wrapped. *You were burned. In a fire. Skin grafts.* He'd shake his head. A little while later, he'd gesture again. I'd repeat. *Fire. Burned. Skin grafts.*

Weighed down, I had to get out of the room to clear my head. I walked back to the waiting room where Bonnie, Matt and Kate waited, where they wondered. *How'd it go?* They asked. *He doesn't get it.* I replied, stunned. By the end of the day, around 5 pm, I'd told Bill seven times that Emma had died. Each time waited for the dam to break, for the tears to come. Nothing. He still hadn't understood. Exhaustion overtook me. I needed to go home. Bonnie said she'd stay after I left so no one else could tell Bill about Emma. That was my job.

JOURNAL ENTRY
March 22, 2005
Day twenty

Well, I told Bill about Emma today. I really don't think it registered at all. He mouthed his response, "no kidding" and "wow". Not at all of what I was expecting. I wonder what tomorrow will bring?

Bill tried to tell me that I looked tired and should go home to rest. It amazes me that he was thinking about me through this.

Lord God, how do I grieve Emma's death? It's so confusing to miss Emma and yet feel normal— even happy—because Bill is doing better.

Please protect him, Abba. Help him to absorb information as he needs and not all at one time.

Help all of us that way. I think Kelsey, Dana and I might be heading into denial—which isn't a good thing.

It still feels like Emma should be coming home to me any day—certainly doesn't feel real yet.

I wonder when that happens?

There have been moments when it felt very real. I don't think I'm in one of those right now.

Help me to grieve, Jesus. Help me to be sad when I need and be joyful at other times. Don't let me run ahead of You or Bill.

But I miss Emma. My heart feels so heavy for her. I don't know what to do.

Please give her a big squeeze for me.

I love you, Emma.

I love you, Jesus.

The next day I returned to the hospital. Bonnie was there with news. A few family members had shown up, wanted to see Bill. Some were upset because I hadn't called to say not to come. Another tried to sneak in to see him.

I just don't get that. Well, in a way I do. Sure, they wanted to see Bill awake, to have that moment with him because he lived. I get that.

But that wasn't the time. It was for me and Bill, mourning, to absorb the news about our daughter...together. It's funny how different people respond in grief. Not funny, *ha ha*, but funny, kind of interesting. Intriguing. Enlightening.

Seth, one of the teaching pastors at Christ Community at that time, gave a message not too long before the fire. In his message he held up a donut. Sugar-coated, I think. But you couldn't tell what was on the inside. Was it jelly? Lemon? Crème-filled? Only one way to find out.....squeeze it. So he did. Jelly oozed between his fingers.

His point? You can't tell what's on the inside of the donut until it gets squeezed....and you can't totally tell what's on our inside until we get squeezed. How does that happen? Trials. Hardships. The insides come out when our capacity to cover up goes away; when our masks are removed and we have no more energy to hide. We, and all the world, see what we're really made of, whether we like it or not.

I learned what was inside of me those first weeks after the fire. More than I expected. More of God than I realized. But I'd worked hard at it, trusted

God during smaller tough times, studied His Word, and talked with Him constantly. Practice? Perhaps. But I believe since I allowed God to have access to my heart, my insides—the deepest parts—He shone brightly those days and weeks and months since the fire. And He continues to do so even now.

For others, the insides weren't quite so bright. Selfishness. Slander. Spewed anger and bitterness. All I asked was for them to wait. To be patient...

I walked into Bill's room that Wednesday morning. A little less prepared to tell him. A little less sure how he would respond. People continued to pray that day, just as they had the day before. What came was totally unexpected and heart-wrenching.

With all my planning, the way Bill finally learned about Emma's death was flippant. I was frustrated. He kept asking the same questions over and over. My patience wore a little thin. I'd already told him several times that second day that Emma had died. I needed him to get it, to catch up so we could mourn together. In the middle of explaining the devastation of the fire...again...I described how we'd lost everything...again...tried to get him to understand what he couldn't see...again. And then I said it. *We lost everything....including Emma.*

What happened next will be forever etched in my mind. Bill's eyes opened wide and he started screaming. Have you ever heard a man with a tracheotomy scream? There's no sound. But I heard the pain. It screamed louder than any noise he could've made. His mouth opened wide as he silently screamed for his little girl. Tears poured from his eyes. The sound of his shattering heart filled the room.

He got it this time.

Once again I begged God to spare him, to save him, to give him the strength to endure.

Chapter 10
Waiting and Dreaming

"The secret to longevity is to keep breathing." Sophie Tucker

Those days after I told Bill about Emma's death were often a blur; one moment blended into another until each memory jumbles with another. During those days I started journaling again, kept track of my thoughts and my feelings as well as the events of what happened. So I could remember...

JOURNAL ENTRY
March 23, 2005
Day twenty-one

It is still so difficult to comprehend everything that is happening. Every morning I wake up and have to remind myself that Emma is not alive—that my house is totally gone—and Bill is still at Loyola. I can't work because other thoughts occupy my mind.

My house. All our stuff—collectables, toys, heir-loom jewelry. They're all gone. That is difficult to understand—at least it's hard to understand the magnitude.

I know I shouldn't go down this path but what if I had slowed down that morning? If I had just taken a little more time to get ready, I could've done something about the fire—at least gotten Bill and Emma out of the house.

Lord God, it hurts so much. I think of Emma running on the beach in Florida last July, totally carefree. I had beautiful pictures of her and now they're gone. That makes me mad! I realize that this is part of your plan but couldn't something special like that been saved?!

My head, and a part of my heart, does understand for the sake of the neighbors but I miss Emma. Please help me keep the big picture in front of me. Please use this tragedy in my life for good in some-one else's life. Multiply the good to ease my hurt. Help me to get through today without my Emma.

You are bigger than this entire situation. You do not intend to hurt me—only to give me a hope and a future (Jeremiah 29:11). Keep my eyes fo-cused on you, Jesus. Write my story so I can tell others about you.

I love you, Emma.

I love you, Jesus.

———

JOURNAL ENTRY
March 25, 2005
Day twenty-three

"I will extol the Lord at all times; His praise will always be on my lips. My soul will boast in the Lord; let the afflicted hear and rejoice. Glorify the Lord with me; let us exalt His name together." (Psalm 34:1-3 NIV)

Lord God, I do praise you. I have lost so much— more than I ever thought I could handle—yet now I realize what's true. All of it boils down to having a relationship with you.

My heart hurts, though, Jesus. It is shattered in so many pieces—more than I know how to put back together—more than I could handle on my own.

I miss Emma so deeply that I am numb. I know what's true but I still feel numb. Too much stuff to absorb. Trying to help Bill recover while still beginning to process and grieve.

Jesus, it hurts so much that I will never see Emma again, this side of heaven. I miss her hugs, her I love you's, her running to our bed in the middle of the night.

There are times I wish you didn't make me as you did. I wish that you chose to allow Emma to live. I know you know how much I love Emma—yet you love her so much more.

Do you give her hugs and kisses? Is she okay in heaven with you? I wish I knew for sure—I guess that's faith.

Please squeeze her and tell her how much she is loved and missed.

I love you, Emma!

I love you, Jesus!

———— ♦ ————

JOURNAL ENTRY
March 26, 2005
Day twenty-four

Today I heard Bill's voice for the first time since the fire. Thank you, Lord! I know I prayed that your will be done but I'm so grateful that you chose to spare Bill's life so we could travel this road together.

I will admit how surreal it all still feels—it's weird. I know Emma died. I can say the words and under-stand it with my head—I'm just not sure about my heart. It all feels wrong—like I'm in a dream.

It did feel a little more real when we were shopping tonight. Realizing I won't buy any more clothes or shoes or toys for Emma. Nothing. And to think I won't see her doing handstands or flips or simply jumping around the room—I just don't get it. Denial? Maybe I am. It's hard to say.

I do know I miss her. Oh Emma, I miss you so much! To a point, I don't know how to live without you. I know I did, before you were born. But you totally changed my life. You were my baby—my child with my husband. You were my blessing. Part of me doesn't know how to move on from here. How do I live without you?

So how is heaven? Have you met some friends and family? How was meeting Jesus? Did you run and give him a big hug?

I so wish I could give you a big squeeze. I miss you so much. I am so sad without you.

Daddy is doing better. He misses you, too. We love you and can't wait to see you again.

Jesus, thank you for loving my Emma. Please take good care of her. Let her know how much I love her and miss her.

I can't believe this is real.

Bill was transferred to a rehabilitation facility in downtown Chicago twenty-seven days after the fire destroyed our home, brought devastation to our lives. Twenty-seven days of living without Emma. Twenty-seven days of waiting for Bill to come home. But not yet. He needed to keep moving forward, to learn to walk and to breathe without any assistance. Unfortunately, a slight accident kept him at Loyola one day longer than planned.

I'd just arrived to visit him that morning. He'd moved out of the burn unit into a regular room. But when I walked in, he wasn't there. What I saw freaked me out...there was blood...on his pillow. My breath caught in my throat.

What happened this time?

As I took a deep breath...seconds passed and an orderly rolled Bill in. Apparently, he'd fallen in the bathroom, thought he could go in on his own. After three weeks of unconsciousness, immobile, in bed. With severely burned legs...and skin grafts. Needless to say, he was a little weak, got a tad lightheaded, and went down for the count. Falling, his head hit the edge of the shower. A nurse checked on him, found him sprawled on the floor. They ordered an MRI to make sure there wasn't any additional damage.

Bill wanted life to return to normal but didn't allow his body to catch up, to heal. He pushed forward like he'd never been burned, that the fire never happened. But it did. The fire did happen and he was injured. Badly. And Emma did die.

Reality, quite frankly...sucks.

I decided to take Dana and Kelsey downtown for a sort of vacation, a shopping spree and, more importantly, to be close to Bill at the rehabilitation center. The drive back and forth from my parents' house exhausted me. I needed to do slow down, at least for the week of spring break.

That trip was odd. At times it felt completely normal. The insurance company had given us some money to hold us over, to replace things and enough for housing. Why not choose a nice hotel off Michigan Avenue? After all, it was a short walk from there to where Bill worked through rehab. For the first time as a family, I was able to get things the girls wanted without worrying too much about money, within reason. We shopped for books and clothes, searched for special memories of Emma. We found Emma's birthstone rings for the girls, a double heart necklace for me.

But it seemed that every place I turned I saw her, or reminders of the fire. A burning smell sent me back to that first morning, the stench in my hair. A walk along Michigan Avenue brought us near the American Girl Place, memories of Emma's *best-*

est day of her entire life...and it was. It hurt to simply see the building as recollections of that day swirled through every thought in my mind. Tears pooled to the verge of spilling as swarms of girls on spring break paraded with dolls in their arms.

My little girl would never hold her doll again, and now my arms were empty, too.

JOURNAL ENTRY
April 3, 2005
Day thirty-three

I am amazed at how life seems to continue—actually does continue—even when it feels like the world should stop and mourn with us.

This past week was good in one sense—the girls and I got a little break while hanging out in Chicago. It was bad because we eventually had to return to reality.

Emma isn't with us anymore.

The house is destroyed.

Bill isn't back yet.

Reality is so hard. It hurts. It's very sad. Good thing it includes you, Jesus. Reality is also that Emma is with you. Reality is that you love us and are taking care of us. Reality is that you are in control. Reality is that I want you to be glorified and honored.

Despite the reality of my pain, missing Emma so much I can't even cry.

Thank you for always being with us. Thank you for carrying me through my worst nightmare. I want to question you...why Emma? Why me?

Why not?

I know that you are in control. You are letting people know about you. It's all part of your plan. Who can argue with you? Who has the right to question you?

I just need help with the pain. I need your comfort as I live my life without Emma.

Oh Emma, I miss you. I love you so much—more than the whole world and everything in it.

I just miss her.....

Bill came home from rehab about ten days after he'd been admitted. The staff trained me how to care for his burns, change his dressings, slough away the dead flesh. But then again, we weren't really home. The four of us, Bill, me, Kelsey and Dana lived with my parents. In two bedrooms.

How was it all going to work? What would life be like now that everyone was back together, everyone who was still alive, that is?

Only Emma was missing. Our family would never be whole again. An empty place at our table. A quieter house. A broken heart.

How would we survive?

JOURNAL ENTRY
April 5, 2005
Day thirty-six

"Fear not, for I am with you; be not dismayed, for I am your God. I will strengthen you, yes, I will help you, I will uphold you with my righteous right hand."
Isaiah 41:10

Abba, my heart aches for Emma. It's still so difficult to believe she's gone.

It's weird—my day wasn't too bad but now I'm having a difficult night. It didn't help to hear someone say what Bill is going through is harder than anything we've gone through.

I'm tired of hearing things like that. It was said about the stroke, too. He makes it sound like what I've gone through is nothing. That my pain and suffering doesn't matter.

Who knows.

I'm tired. It's late. And I'm mad that I don't have Emma anymore. I'm tired of people judging me or my actions. I wish people would just leave me alone.

Oh Emma, my heart breaks for you. I miss you so much—bigger than the universe. I wish you were here.

I love you, Stinkerpot.

Are there toots in heaven?

Please let me know, somehow, that you're okay.

Fill my emptiness, Jesus. Help me through this.

Strengthen me for the tough road ahead.

JOURNAL ENTRY
April 7, 2005
Day thirty-eight

My heart continues to break. I miss Emma so much. But I know I'm not the only one. Unfortunately, my hurt is coming across as irritation, annoyance. I'm just plain mad at the world.

I hate the fact that Emma is not here anymore. I hate having to watch Kelsey go through so much pain and agony and not know what to do. I hate the fact that my house is gone. I hate it all. I hate the fact that extended family have responded as they have—most concern showered on Bill—none for me. Then I get dumped on—can't make decisions without people getting angry.

Lord God, I'm just feeling mad. Why can't our life be somewhat normal?! Why can't all my kids have lived? I guess I am struggling with the why.

I don't want to hurt. I don't want to live life without my Emma. It isn't fair. Why us? Why did you choose us to deal with this?

Yes, to glorify you.

But at the cost of my five-year-old daughter? I'm not sure. I don't want to deny you—I will not—but I wish you'd chosen someone else.

I want Emma with me.

I miss you, Emma. I love you. Always.

JOURNAL ENTRY
April 9, 2005
Day forty

Oh Abba, I need your strength right now. I need your comfort. I need you. My heart still breaks for Emma. Today Bill and I saw her at Conley's Funeral Home. It was his first time seeing her since the fire.

It was my second.

The day had come. We'd waited for the final service...the burial...until Bill was out of the hospital. I figured it wasn't enough just to have the service; he had to see her...in the casket...to make it real for him.

Oh how I hated the thought of that day.

Not because Bill would see her; well, maybe a little. Really because I was about to see her...again. When we arrived at Conley's Funeral Home, Bruce sat with us. He explained to Bill what he would see. They had the casket set open, in one of their rooms, just for me and Bill, her parents, to finally grieve together.

But I couldn't go in right away. It took everything in me to even show up at the funeral home, let alone walk inside. Once again I focused on my breathing, the simple act of inhaling and exhaling. I had to think about something else, something other than what I was about to see. I sobbed, uncontrollably. The protection of shock was long gone. This time I knew exactly what had happened, what I

- 131 -

would see. Bruce told me in all the years of serving grieving families, he'd never had someone see a loved one a second time.

Figures.

Bruce allowed us to take our time. He gave me permission to proceed slowly...at one point I wasn't even sure I could do it, see her again. Her body. I'd stepped out on the porch as Bill stood before Emma's casket, stroked her hair...struggled to breathe. Minutes passed until I was able to move next to him, heart racing...palms sweating. And then together, as Emma's mommy and daddy, we cried. We whispered of our love...forever. And then we said goodbye, one final time.

———————

JOURNAL ENTRY
April 9, 2005
Day forty-one

My heart hurts so much today. Lord God, I said I would be willing to bear this cross of living my life without Emma. I can only do this with your strength. I am too weak on my own.

I'm beginning to question your love. I feel like all I get is your discipline. Oh how I long to feel your love—to be enveloped by it—surrounded by it— overwhelmed by it.

I know you love me but now I'm really questioning it because you allowed Emma to die. My worst nightmare—what am I supposed to do? How am I to live without her?

It was so much more real to see her (body) again yesterday. The shock of the first few days is gone... it so was different to see her this time. She looked more like her, and yet not totally real, because she wasn't breathing, wasn't really there. She's with you. It's so hard to truly comprehend that yesterday will be the last time I will ever see her on earth.

I think I'm losing sight of eternity. I feel like I'm sinking into a pit. Life goes on for everyone except me. I will never have a normal life. Kelsey will never grow up with a normal life. Am I destined for heartbreak?

I still can't believe Bill and I haven't even been married for eight years—and look at all we've gone through.

Abba, help me. I need you. I need to stand firm—help me not to waiver—help me to endure life without my precious Emma.
Oh Emma, I miss you so much. You always brought me joy. You made my heart smile. Help it to smile again one day. Help me live without you.

I love you.

Always.

———————

JOURNAL ENTRY
April 14, 2005
Day forty-five

Oh Jesus, the pain is incredible—almost unbearable. I don't know what to do. I don't know how to respond. People keep telling me what an inspiration I am...how strong I am. I don't want to be. I don't want to live my life without having Emma with me. I don't want to live without ever seeing her smile again, or see her face light up, hear her tell me how much she loves me.

It feels so unfair...so horrible...so very unbelievable.

Oh Emma, I miss your smile. I miss watching you play with your ponies. I miss hearing your voice. I miss feeling your hugs. I miss how you played with my hair—how you'd ask me to do that and then tell me that you always do that. I miss having you sleep in "your spot" between me and Daddy. I miss fixing you a taco, a bowl of chocolate cereal, of getting your drink of milk. I miss making sure you brushed all of your teeth, hearing your quiet breathing as you slept.

Emma, I don't want to live without you. I miss you. I want you back with me. I don't want to bury your precious body on Saturday. I don't want people to forget about you. I don't want to wait until heaven to see you again.

And yet, I have no choice. It's been six weeks of living without you. Six long, terrible weeks. The pain is incredible. The loss is indescribable. The suffering acute. I don't want to be strong. I want you with me. I don't want to be an inspiration—I want you to be alive here on earth.

Oh Abba, help me. Take this pain away. Make this all a terrible nightmare. I want to wake up.

But then I wonder—so many people prayed for Emma. You could have chosen to save her, to heal her. But you didn't. You chose to let her die. How do I reconcile that? How do I go on knowing you chose to leave me on earth without my baby? Part of me wants to demand an explanation. But then I understand that your ways are higher than my ways and your thoughts are than my thoughts. I have no business demanding anything.

And yet I hurt. More than any other time in my life. Are you really weeping for me? With me? Do you even care? This was the one thing I asked you to never have me go through. I can't believe my Emma died in a house fire.

Are you asking me to be obedient? If I obey, like Abraham, will you bring her back to me? I don't know how to respond to you. My head tells me one thing but my heart tells me something else.

How do I do this? I wish there were a roadmap—a way to navigate. Are you real? Is heaven real? Is Emma really there? I need your assurance, your love, your comfort.

I'm just feeling confused right now. Please help me to see clearly, to trust you and to have faith that there will be good. Lots of good.

Good night precious Emma. I love you.

JOURNAL ENTRY
April 15, 2005
Day forty-six

In less than twelve hours we'll bury Emma's body. I don't want to sleep. Right now I don't want to face tomorrow. I want today to last forever so I don't have to move on without my baby.

Lord God, it hurts. The pain is unbearable. I don't know how to move on—to carry on. I don't want to live my life without Emma.

And yet, Emma lived her full life. For some reason you chose a short five years for Emma to live. She was complete. My heart wants to scream in rebellion—to tell you it's not true…it's not possible…this cannot be real.

But it is.

Reality, too, is how you are providing for our needs.

But I don't have Emma.

———————

JOURNAL ENTRY
April 16, 2005
Day forty-seven

We buried Emma today. Six weeks after it all happened. My heart still hurts—I miss my sweet girl so much.

But I choose to praise you, Jesus. I praise you for your love. I praise you for your care. I praise you for never leaving me…or Emma.

Thank you for the strength today. Thank you for surrounding me with people who love you…and who love me. Thank you for not allowing us to endure this pain alone.

Today the tears were healing. I don't want to say goodbye to Emma—but I don't have a choice. Apparently, this is your will. Help me to have faith to see it through. Help me to endure life without my Princess Emma. Help me to honor you in my response to all that is happening. May my sacred sorrow be worship to you.

I love you, Emma. Have fun in heaven until I see you again. Please don't forget about me. I love you bigger than my pain.

Chapter 11
Feelings Following Emma's Death

"Whenever I feel blue, I start breathing again." L. Frank Baum

How can I describe what it feels like after the death of a child? How do I explain the devastation, the despair, the rollercoaster of emotions, the confusion, the darkness? And then there are the glimpses of hope and joy, the peace that passes all understanding, all in the midst of such incredible sorrow.

I'm not quite sure anyone can truly understand. But perhaps a glimpse...

JOURNAL ENTRY
April 20, 2005
Day fifty-one

Lord God, I miss Emma so much. I can't believe I'm living without her. My heart wants my body to be devastated, yet it's not. My heart is broken but my spirit is intact.

I wonder if the reality of it all has truly sunk in. Saturday, the day we buried her, was very real. Very final. Very sad. Overwhelming. Is my mind protecting me a bit from completely understanding and accepting what has happened? Does it come in waves?

My conflict is that somehow my soul is joyful. I'm not happy—I'm in a state of joy. It's not a feeling but I can't completely describe it. Assurance? Peace. It has to be from you. Thank you.

But, oh, how I miss her! I wish I could see her...hold her...feel one of her squeezes, arms wrapped tight around my neck. If I had my choice, I would not be living my life without her. I don't know how.

What is heaven like, Emma? Have you met David? Has he told you about your favorite story...when he fought Goliath? And Abraham? Elijah? Grandma's sister? I wish I could talk to you. To catch a glimpse of what you're experiencing. A taste. I feel so lost without you. Who is taking care of you? Do you sleep at all? Is there night and day? Are you playing? Learning? Are you lonely? Do you miss me? Do you think about me at all?

I wish you were here. I want you with me. I want to hold you and care for you. I want to be your mommy on earth. I don't want it to be over. I need you here with me. It hurts. There is such a void in my life. I don't know with what to fill it.

Comfort me, Abba. For whatever reason you chose to call Emma to yourself. I don't understand why but I'm choosing to trust you. I don't know how to live without Emma but I'm choosing to follow you. Comfort my broken heart. Please give me your peace, Jesus, the peace that passes all understanding. Continue to bless me with joy— unexplainable joy knowing you are completely in control. I have nothing to fear. Nothing to be ashamed of. Nothing to worry about.

Keep my marriage together. Help us to reach out to one another. To talk about Emma, the fire, how we're feeling. Put hedges up so neither of us is tempted.

Please protect Kelsey, too. Heal her broken heart. Please encourage Kelsey to hang out with her friends. To reach out. To not be alone.

Give Emma a big squeeze, Jesus.

Tell her I love her and I miss her so much.

JOURNAL ENTRY
May 1, 2005
Day sixty-one

Well, this is the last day at my parents' house. Tomorrow we move into our temporary housing until our new house is built.

I don't want to go.

I don't want to move on without my Emma—my baby.

And yet I know I have no choice. Just as I had no choice when I became pregnant with her, I now have no choice to live on this earth without her.

Oh Abba, I don't want the days to pass because I feel like I'm moving away from her; that life will feel like she never lived—that she was just a dream.

Why did you have to let this happen? Why my baby? Why my family? It hurts so bad—I don't know how I will ever get through this.

I ache to see her—I don't want this. I told you it would break me—and it is. This is destroying me and I can't go on. I know I should be comforted that she is in your presence, but today I'm not. I want her to be here…with me.

My heart is crushed.

Emma will never grow up with us. Kelsey will never be able to play with Emma again. I feel like I'm losing—and have lost—everything. I am broken and so terribly alone.

Am I losing hope?

I think so. This is too difficult. I don't know how to make it through. I feel like giving up, letting it all go and not care about anything anymore.

And yet I know you love me. At least I know that is true in my head. My heart is so crushed and empty it's hard to understand. How is your love in this tragedy? Reveal yourself, I beg you. Reveal yourself in my own heart. Help me to feel your love, your power, your strength. Carry me through this pain, Lord Jesus. Restore and mend my broken heart so I might be used to bring you glory.

I need you. I want to draw closer to you but I'm afraid. I'm afraid at what you'll take from me again. I'm afraid I got it all wrong. Please reveal yourself to me. Put my feet on solid rock. Hold me so I don't stumble. Keep me from failing.

Bring good from the midst of this pain and sorrow.

I choose to believe you are close to the brokenhearted. I choose to believe that you will redeem this for your glory. I choose to believe you are carrying me through on wings of eagles. I choose to believe you love me, even when I don't feel it.

I choose to believe you have a plan for my life, one that is not to harm me but to give me hope and a future. I believe you are in control. I believe

Emma is with you in heaven and, one day, I will see her again. I choose to believe she is safe in your presence, in your arms, Jesus, even thought I don't understand and my heart is shattered.

I choose to follow you, despite how I feel right now. I choose to trust you despite not knowing where you are leading me. I choose to obey you, just like Abraham, even though I don't know where I'm going.

I choose to believe but I still have to deal with my feelings. As a mom, help me when my arms ache to hold my little girl. As a mom, help me when I long to hear her voice say, I love you. As a mom, help me survive when the wave of emotion threatens to overwhelm me, to overtake me, to sink me.

Please forgive me for my selfishness, for my anger, and self-centeredness. Thank you for sparing Bill's life. Please protect our marriage and make it stronger than it was before.

Help me to walk through the valley of the shadow of death. Carry me when I'm weary. I cast all my fears, my anxieties, my concerns and my sadness on you.

Use me as you see fit. Do what you will—lead me and guide me. Holy Spirit, keep me on the straight and narrow. Don't let me move to the left or the right. Help me to forgive where I need to forgive.

Do not let my enemies triumph over me as my hope is in you. Cleanse my soul of any yuck that keeps me from you, Lord God.

Today Kelsey stood in front of 1300 people through baptism and declared that she would follow you. Oh, Jesus, thank you. I pray she would learn and grow from this. I pray her hunger for your Word would dominate. Lead Kelsey. Protect her. May she grow to be a woman after your own heart.

Please tell Emma I love her so much. Squeeze her and kiss her for me. Tell her I miss her but trust I will see her again one day. Please don't let her forget me.

Help me to make it through this sorrow. Help me to be content—no matter how I feel. Fill me with joy so others will want you in their lives. Help me to be a shining light for you.

But could you let me know that Emma is okay? I believe you can do that—you have all the power to do whatever you desire. Please let me know, somehow. Whether through peace, a picture or a dream, I need your blessed assurance that my little baby is safe in your arms.
I love you, Emma, bigger than the universe. And I will love you, always and forever. I will never forget you nor allow your life to be a waste.

I love you!

I've often had people tell me I seem okay with Emma's death...the fire. They think I'm over it. Healed. Restored. Or...completely delusional.

I suppose it depends on the day.

There are some days when I do feel at peace with life. "It is well....with my soul" to borrow words from a well-known hymn.

On those days I feel I'm truly trusting in God's sovereign plan. My eyes fixed on the big picture. I know Emma is completely safe—fire cannot touch her precious little body, nothing more can hurt her. God gives me glimpses of his goodness, His breath of fresh wind upon my cheek. It is well.

But then I have other types of days, hard ones. Flashbacks of the fire. Hearing a little girl crying for her mommy. I never heard Emma that morning. But the sound haunts me...at a store, the mall, church. A little voice cries and I wonder.

I wonder about Emma's last moments on earth. Was she crying out for me? For her daddy? Did she know what was happening; see the flames around her...the smoke? Was she wondering where her family was? Why we weren't there to save her?

And that final moment, her last breath...was she afraid? Did terror fill her tender heart? Or peace? Was Jesus there?

When people watch me and see a smile or a bounce in my step, do they see the real me? Or am I hiding? Truth be told, I'm not sure how many people could truly handle the truth. Would they really want to know my thoughts? Is it really appropriate to share?

I tried that early on. The day of the fire, in fact. There had been some conflict in our extended family— like so many other families. I clearly remember looking at two of the guys involved. I shared my heart—*if nothing else, something good has come from this tragedy*. They were in the same room... together.

But it didn't last.

Sometimes it seems better to keep my thoughts to myself. There's a time and a place to share and only with certain people, safe ones. Those who will listen without judgment, without wondering what my role may have been in the fire. Who will sit and just be, and let me be...no expectations, no comments, and no quick exits because the pain is too hard for them to hear.

Imagine if we walked around, our thoughts and feelings displayed for all to see. Every idea, every sorrow, every frustration, every lie exposed. Could the world handle that? Could our friends? Our family? Could we?

Yet we look at each other during the course of an interaction and judge: *Oh, she's smiling. Life must be good.* Or, *why does she keep wearing that mask? Why doesn't she just cry? Let it all out?*

Because if the tears start to flow, I fear they'll never stop.

But then why can't someone smile simply because God is good, despite what difficult circumstances are happening, even in the midst of it? "Keep your eyes fixed on Jesus, the Author and Perfecter of our faith..." (Hebrews 12:2) On days when I'm questioning life and death and suffering, God's Word reminds me to turn my eyes away from that yuck and focus on the One who is in control; who not only knows my story but loves me and allows me to co-write my story with Him.

He helps me to breathe in those moments when sadness and despair threaten to overtake my soul. When I want to cry out to everyone.....*of course I miss Emma*! Of course I'd rather be curled up in bed with the covers over my head; pretend this has been some dream...a horrible nightmare!

But I can't. I can't give up. I have to keep breathing. In and out....in and out. Trusting that there's something more. Hoping that this isn't all there is to life; there really is something beyond what we can see. Believing that God has a plan and a purpose for this devastation that has transformed me. A chance to learn with each passing breath.

Time has taken on new meaning. In one sense, it has stood still. Yes, the clock ticks and days pass, months, even years. But every time I look at Emma's picture, time has stopped. She doesn't grow, doesn't change. Forever five.

Then I walk around church, see kids her age and somehow time speeds up again. Fast forwards as kids have entered Kindergarten, First grade... Second...Third...Fourth. Baby teeth replaced by grown up ones. Books read. Sports played. So much difference.

I still picture Emma with her ponies, watching her favorite movies...Disney princesses, Barbie, Spirit, Brother Bear. Time has frozen, and yet somehow... it still moves on...without her.

I've thought about age-progression technology. Submit a picture to see what she'd look like now. At each birthday to somehow watch her grow. Keep her alive.

But, I can't. She's not here. Because she'll never grow beyond age five. She'll never lose her teeth or go to school or learn to read. She'll never meet a boy, have a broken heart or know the joy of falling deeply in love. She'll never learn to drive or play tennis or take gymnastics like we'd planned.

But if I could just see her one more time...moving...alive. Certainly that would be heaven...just here on earth.

———

JOURNAL ENTRY
May 7, 2005
Day sixty-seven

The pain never seems to stop. The intensity. The sadness. The emptiness. My cries rip from the depth of my soul. So deep yet without tears.

I went to visit Emma's grave yesterday. It looked so small...and alone. I didn't like being there. I miss Emma too much.

But I did dream about her last night. She seemed real. She moved. She smiled—at me. It was my first dream of her since the fire.

Thank you, Abba. It soothed my heart to see her... almost normal. Thank you for the hope I felt this morning when I woke up. Not hope that she would come home but hope that you are still in control.

Please help me to remember that. Help me to keep my eyes fixed on you. I want to stay close to you. Help me to stand strong. Please forgive me for doubting you, for thinking you don't love me.

I know you do.

I want to continue to obey you, to follow you even though I don't know where I'm going. Help me to be like Abraham. I want to finish this race....

Chapter 12
Me & Bill

"The world breaks everyone. Then some become strong at the broken places."
Ernest Hemingway

People often ask how Bill and I are doing since Emma's death...or, rather, since the fire, as many people shy away from mentioning *Emma* and *death* in the same sentence. Truth be told, I don't always know how to respond.

How do you describe the ripping that occurs when a child dies? The sheer fabric of your heart torn to shreds? The intense pain and uncertainty that consumes your soul? How is it possible to then coexist with another person when you can barely breathe yourself?

Honestly, sometimes I think people just want to hear that everything's okay. That life is back to normal because...well...that's easier, less messy. They want to know that people survive this kind of stuff. They need a sense of hope.

But that's not life. Sometimes it does hurt. A lot.

Especially after betrayal. Next to Emma's death, I think that hurt the most. My husband, the one to whom I pledged love and honor till death, truly wrestled to figure out if I'd purposely and intentionally attempted to take his life....and succeeded with Emma.

Seriously.

I'll never forget the moment I heard what he and several extended family members thought—that I had the capacity for such destruction. I was with Matt at his work attempting to figure out why Bill seemed distant, more than the result of Emma's death. More than grief. Something was brewing, but I couldn't quite put my finger on it.

Matt looked right at me, eyes wide, breathing quickly. He wouldn't tell me. Couldn't tell me. But he knew. He stated that if what people said was true, it was bad, really bad.

My mind raced as I tried to process. What could be so bad? Emma already died. We'd already faced some possibilities of the cause of the fire... none were arson, a fire started on purpose. What could it be?

Finally, Matt relented. *They think it's you.* Another day, another conversation. ME?! You have got to be kidding. I was shocked, stunned, to say the least. It almost felt like I was in front of my house again, watching as it burned with Bill and Emma inside...helpless.

I knew there was some internal struggle with Dana, how she felt. There'd been concern since Emma's celebration service, when she disappeared with friends. And then a phone call to church from a concerned parent. A rumor circulated around school that Dana was afraid she'd started the fire, with a cigarette. But when the fire investigators talked with her, she denied everything, including smoking, regardless of the cigarette butts shoved between the mattress and box spring of her bed. I asked one of the investigators if it was just a fire waiting to happen. He said yes...only it was Emma who died.

But to think that Emma died because of me? On purpose? I didn't know how to respond. It was an absolute lie. I did not purposely and intentionally start the fire. No one did. The fire was an accident, a horrible accident.

After talking with Matt I left. In tears. Shock. Betrayal. I called Larry, my brother-in-law, hysterical, driving a car. Not a good combination. But I didn't know what to do. How does one respond after that kind of accusation?

Murder? Me?

Apparently, according to distant family, this wasn't even my first attempt. The first was Bill's stroke. Wow. I'm good? And what was I to gain? Money? I don't think so; we were two single parents who got married. Notoriety? Fame? Nope. Their reasoning: a paranoid schizophrenic, or possibly a new house. I wasn't even sure what exactly that meant.

Once again, I tried to figure it all out, my new way of life. During this time, Dana had gone into the city with some of those family members. She was supposed to come home one day, but ended up staying a few days longer, without our knowledge or approval. She was still a minor, only 17. Together, Bill and I decided that he would drive to Chicago and pick her up, bring her home. We talked. We planned. He would walk in, get her, and walk out. I set up a meeting with a counselor. For Dana's care. For ours.

Hours passed.

I called his cell. *Where are you?* I asked. Still in the city, he replied. *You need to come home.* Soon, he said. I waited some more. *Why aren't you leaving yet?* They were still talking. That wasn't part of the plan. I waited longer, with my sister-in-law, Kate. And then finally, hours later, he came home. Without Dana. A different plan set in motion. A family member drove her to her mom's house. We went on to the counselor without her.

What did you talk about? I was curious...he'd been gone so long. Nothing, he assured me. *For hours? You didn't talk about anything?* No, it's not your business, his tone tight. *But you were gone for a long time. How did you not talk about anything?* What, are you paranoid?

No idea what was coming.

The truth, or rather the accusations, trickled out over the following weeks, and even months. The lies with which they filled Bill's head...the twisting of my words and actions. Why did I go home that morning of the fire? Why didn't I go inside to get her, to rescue him? Why had I told Emma if something ever happened and she was scared, to go to our neighbor's house? Why did I tell Kelsey in the burn unit that it was just me and her again, when Bill was still in a coma, alive? Why did I ignore Bill after he came home? Why didn't I let anyone visit him? Why? Why? Why?

Life was already hard enough, trying to live, to function. But now? The betrayal? I wanted to run. To quit. To give up. Those accusations were nothing but lies, yet they threatened to obliterate my already damaged family. They split us, squeezed us, and exposed everything inside.

And then it came...a gift of strength in the form of a movie, or rather a series of movies. We watched a lot of movies at the townhouse, our temporary housing while our new home was built. A luxury, I know. But those stories served as a distraction from reality. Emma didn't need me anymore, nor did the house or even any animals. Matt lived with his mom. Dana came and went, depending on the day. Bill retreated into himself, and the computer. Kelsey and I were left to ourselves, tried to function in the midst of deep sorrow, to breathe in a new place. So our attention turned to others, different drama, many with a happy ending because we didn't have ours.

During that time we watched the Lord of the Rings trilogy. It scared me, especially after seeing death in real life. But truth rang out from those movies. Truth that hit me square between the eyes and truly changed the course of our marriage.

Two scenes—one occurred in the beginning, the other towards the end. A brief sketch: the main character, Frodo, on a quest to return a ring that had magical powers, evil powers. A group of warriors committed to help him, a few trusted friends. Sam was one.

Early in the story, Sam tried to take the ring from Frodo, to help him, to give him a break. Putting it mildly, Sam failed. It wasn't his job, Frodo explained. The ring was his burden to carry, not Sam's.

Fast forward towards the end of the trilogy. Sam and Frodo, after incredible adventure and toil, closed in on their destination. But Frodo felt he couldn't make it. Beyond exhausted, he'd been beaten, almost killed, lost, alone, frightened. He had no more energy, no more strength. Sam looked at him with utter devotion and loyalty, his desire deep to help. *I may not be able to carry the burden for you,* Sam told Frodo, *but I can carry you!* Despite his own pain and suffering, Sam picked Frodo up and carried him to the top of the mountain towards success, the completion of their mission.

The question smashed into my heart....if we were in a battle and Bill had been physically hurt, what would I do? Would I abandon him? Turn my back? Look at him and say *oh, you can't take care of me, anymore...good luck!* Walk away?

Absolutely not.

So why, when he'd been so emotionally...and even physically...damaged, would I think it's okay to do the same thing? Because *I* wasn't getting what *I* needed? Because he lashed out at me? Accused me? Because *I* wasn't happy?

Once again, I made a choice to trust. Not Bill, not right away...that trust continues to grow. I chose to trust God, believing that he knew what he was doing, even in my marriage. Even with being accused of such despicable action. Even through betrayal. I refused to let my husband be a casualty in the war we're actually in.

Scripture is clear that there is a battle going on. Only it says that the battle isn't against flesh and blood, against people, it's "against evil rulers and authorities of the unseen world, against mighty powers in this dark world, and against evil spirits in the heavenly places." (Ephesians 6:12)

And it's real. Whether we choose to acknowledge it or not.

I'm not saying that all those accusation were a result of some spirit living inside someone, making him say and do things he didn't want to do. People definitely made choices as to what was said, the accusations. But I did need to realize *they* weren't really the issue. My focus didn't need to stay there. "...for my enemies are waiting for me. Do not let me fall into their hands, for they accuse me of things I've never done; with every breath they threaten me with violence. Yet I am confident I will see the Lord's goodness while I am here in the land of the living." (Psalm 27:11a-13)

In that moment, through that story, God filled me with the strength to stand firm. A determination to fight through prayer. Endurance to persevere through the accusations from my broken husband, to see his pain behind the words, to forgive. And to trust that God had a perfect plan for my life, for Bill's life, for the lives of our kids. Not a plan for me to be happy—for happiness is a feeling that's as fickle as our circumstances, but to experience incredible joy, to be molded and shaped to look more like Jesus.

Don't be fooled. I'm not perfect. These words don't negate what continued to happen: more struggle, more tears, more fights, and more moments when I wanted it all to stop. There were plenty of all, and moments when it still happens. But Bill and I have both chosen to trust God with our marriage, to work diligently to honor the commitment we made before our Father in heaven, even when it was sometimes only that commitment that held us together. We love each other... deeply. Sometimes our hurts get in the way so we try not to allow our feelings control us...no matter what. But it's been hard. Really hard. There was a lot of pain heaped on an already incredibly painful tragedy. Pain that didn't need to be added but for the choice of a few.

Truthfully, I don't know how to answer the question—how we are. I guess given all the details and the drama, we're surviving. Some days are definitely better than others. Some moments it's hard to comprehend all that's occurred while other seconds threaten to destroy the tenuous balance we've established since that day.

So some days I answer...*we're okay* when I'd rather say *we're hurting...deeply.* Other days I marvel at the grace and forgiveness that fill both of our hearts that bind us together. But I suppose all our lives are like that. Moments when we forgive no matter what has happened, regardless of who was right or wrong or how the other person responded. Seconds pass as a comment goes unanswered, fear of the damage that could be done to a tender relationship. Choices to trust even when we'd rather run.

Then those seconds occur, much like the state just after dreaming and right before waking...seconds when I wonder if this has all been some terrible nightmare and when I wake, I'll feel Emma's warm breath brush against my check or perhaps hear the patter of her feet as she scampers into our room. When her sweet voice calls out to me... "Momma!"

But like so many dreams, as my eyes flutter open and my breathing speeds up, reality grabs my heart. Emma isn't here. The fire really happened. Another day begins as I beg for my faith and belief to grow, to sustain, to carry me through. Breathing...slowly. But steady. Trusting...no matter what.

Chapter 13
Glimpses of Goodness in the Valley

"All I have seen teaches me to trust the creator for all I have not seen."
Ralph Waldo Emerson

JOURNAL ENTRY
March 24, 2005
Day twenty-two

I praise you because you are God. I praise you because you are good. You are faithful to all of your promises. Thank you!

Thank you for sustaining me through my worst nightmare. Thank you for the strength to get through each day without Emma.

Thank you for sacred sorrow. I give you my tears as worship...my fears as worship...my broken heart as worship. Use me—use this entire situation to bring you glory and honor and praise.

Thank you for being near to the brokenhearted—because that's what I am. Broken—just plain shattered.

But your grace—your love—is enough.

I would be lying—in denial—if I said nothing about Emma. Oh Abba, Jesus, my heart yearns for my baby girl. It is very difficult to figure out what I'm going to do without her. She gave me joy. Emma made my heart smile. She made me laugh—sometimes cry—even frustrated. But I love her—and she loved me. How can I be whole without her hugs...her kisses...her giggles?

I almost feel lost. My heart ripped in two.

And then a breath of fresh air—like today. Thank you for showing me such love through my friends and staff at Christ Community. They did an awesome job encouraging me on my birthday today. Everyone went out of their way to minister to me. Thank you for those moments of fresh air.

Help me continue to shine brightly for you. Be honored and glorified.

Squeeze my Emma hello for me.

I miss you, Emma.

It amazes me how much goodness I saw those first weeks and months after Emma's death, after the fire. They were there, and I looked for them. I knew the size of the loss, the devastation. And I believed God was bigger, is bigger. He will balance the yuck. God's Word says that He is good. "How kind the Lord is! How good He is! So merciful, this God of ours!" (Psalm 116:5) Not good, though, by our definition. It's so much bigger than that.

So I looked everywhere for His goodness. I expected it, convinced it'd be there...I just needed to keep my eyes open. I had to take God at His word. If I only believed part of what the Bible said and not all of it...would that make God a liar? Or the Bible inaccurate?

I refused to believe either. I trusted. And continue to.

Like my birthday. A mere twenty-two days after the fire. Bill was still groggy. I'd just told him about Emma a couple days before. I felt pretty crappy, to be honest. My first birthday without Emma. Another year older, another reminder that I didn't have her anymore. I hated that day...at first.

The staff at Christ Community completely surprised me. They presented me with gifts of movies and books in two big baskets. Glimpses of God's goodness that reminded me He cared about my mother's heart. He showered me with love and care that day through gifts and words, through all the cards sent covering me with tender care.

A balm to my shattered heart.

And then the letter. A builder who attended Christ Community emailed our Administration Director to present an offer...to rebuild our home. He and his wife had stood on our property the day after the fire. They stood there and prayed for our family, for their involvement. We didn't know each other. But he sensed God leading him to help, to get involved.

The house that love built.

That first day of the fire, I told whoever would listen that I never wanted to go back to the house, that place of ruin. The second day, I decided I never wanted to leave. We didn't have much left...just memories. Memories of Emma and Kelsey playing in our front yard after a storm, water flooded the trench. *Lake Gunderson*, we called it. The playset in the back. Emma and her sisters swinging. Lady, our Sheltie, bouncing around, herding Emma so she didn't stray too far. The tree we planted the year she was born. The flowers she helped me plant. Her footprints throughout our entire yard.

But the house was destroyed...completely. At first the insurance company wanted us to save the garage...yeah. We chose not to build a house around a garage. It was deemed completely destroyed so all of it had to be replaced.

This builder stated that he'd like to help us...because of his love for God and, as a result, for us. He helped tear it down; it took an entire day in June. We stood and watched our lives be reduced to mere rubble. Then he worked diligently to rebuild... our home...and our lives. Our safety and security. A new place to live, to breathe, to heal.

Another gift of God's goodness appeared that day the house was torn down. Emma's blanket— that special one that had been Kelsey's...then passed on to Emma. It'd been on our bed the morning of the fire. I assumed it was lost, forever. Until that day. One by one, the walls came down; the debris crunched into our basement. And there it sat...right on top of it all. Emma's blanket. The one my college roommate had made for Kelsey, cherished by Emma. A gift.

Others helped, too. People gave their time to paint, to sod, to decorate. Each gift of time a glimmer of God's goodness and support...reminding our family that we weren't alone. That Emma was missed. That people cared.

I stopped counting how many cards we received. Cards arrived at my parents' house, the church, it seemed everywhere we turned. Cards offering sympathy, encouragement, and prayers. Many from people we didn't even know. Neighbors. Friends of friends. Family members of friends. Complete strangers who'd been moved by our story. I'd open a card, look at the name...the financial gift...*I don't know this person.* It overwhelmed and strengthened me. What else can this be but God's goodness?

That summer another precious gift offered; a gift of song. I'd encouraged, perhaps even challenged Cindy to write a song about all that'd happened. A song to honor God and encourage others in the midst of great sorrow. I didn't know she'd taken those words to heart.

Cindy handed me an envelope and told me to look inside when I was alone, at the town home. Being at work may not have been the best place because of the content. But I couldn't wait. So I found a room in the nursery at church, one with a CD player. I opened the envelope and there it was, a CD with that gift of song: *Goodbye for Now.* A song from Cindy's heart. For Emma. For me. And for another dear friend of Cindy's who'd died the exact same day as Emma.

The song was going on her new CD, her first one. Another breath of God's goodness swept over me. This was a gift to be shared with others, because of Emma's gift to us.

And then there were the pictures. Months passed. Summer ended and fall began. We'd moved in our new home, a physical reminder of God's goodness and grace. The few things that had been saved moved from the storage unit to the house. Thirty-two boxes held mementos of our former life.

Some of the boxes held pictures. Pictures of Emma...looking at me as I snapped her picture, freezing that moment with me forever. Pictures of Kelsey as a little girl, family trips to Niagara Falls and the Smoky Mountains.

Looking at those pictures made me wish even more for the ones from our trip to Florida and Disney World. Just a few, I begged God. But I knew it wasn't possible. I'd been scrapbooking those pictures the night before the fire. I'd left them in the family room so they were completely destroyed. No evidence of the joy of that trip. The laughter. The fun.

Or so I thought.

As I looked through the boxes I found a bag of negatives. I'd seen them in the box at the town-house but it overwhelmed me to look through them all. To realize that those pictures were all we had left of Emma, of the earlier years of our life together as a family. It hurt too much.

But one day I kept going, kept looking. I wanted to know what we had, what was left. I opened the bag and held each negative up to the light. I saw pictures of Bill's family, of Matt and Dana. Ones we already had. I was just about done, ready to quit, when I saw it. One of the negatives...a picture of Emma? I held it closer to the light. Were my eyes playing tricks? Was I hallucinating?

No.

I looked at a picture of Emma...at the beach... in Florida. And then another. Emma splashing her older sisters in the Gulf of Mexico. And another... Emma, Kelsey and Dana playing in the water together. And another...and another...thirteen pictures in all. Thirteen examples of God's goodness.

Truthfully, I don't remember separating the negatives from the pictures. The family room had flashed. Everything, including the air, had ignited, burned. There was no possible way for anything to be saved.

The only explanation is that a loving God somehow protected those negatives, those thirteen pictures from our Florida trip. The fire had started in the family room but burned so fast, so hot, that it burned right through the ceiling...the floor of our bedroom. Right where I kept all of our family pictures. Every memory, every photo album, every negative. A hole was left where the floor had been. Every picture should have been destroyed, become ash. But God cared about my heart, my dream, my desire to have a few pictures saved.

When the fire restoration team worked through our home, trying to save what they could, I'd told them about the pictures, exactly where they were in our bedroom and in the closet. The floor had burned all the way to the edge of the bookcase, the one that held our pictures. Just about every picture on that unit was saved. Many others were lost, but not all.

Not even those precious pictures of our trip to Florida. Fourteen total. My dad had one from Disney, the one of Emma and Kelsey taken with Ariel. He'd told me he had it six months after the fire. God's perfect timing. One picture for each part of our trip. Such a precious reminder of that special time...the carefree spirit...the fun. The sheer enjoyment of life lived by all four of us girls.

The day we moved into our new home another treasure arrived. The painting I'd asked my friend Janet to paint—the one of Emma and Jesus, walking away, hand in hand. A vivid reminder of Emma's reality as we continue to live in ours. A gift to mark the day we moved home. A gift to remember...Emma's gift.

———————

JOURNAL ENTRY
October 27, 2005

What a day. From sadness and tears to joy and hope. Thank you for our new home. It is absolutely beautiful. Thank you for your provision. Thank you for calling men to obedience—men like the builder from our church. Thank you for the encouragement I feel from my boss, Larry. Especially when he calls to tell me how beautiful our home is.

And it is beautiful, Lord God. So much more than I ever expected. Thank you for our builder and his employees. Please show me how to properly thank him. He took a huge risk to rebuild our home—then to have so many people donate— thank you. I pray he would continue to be a man after your own heart—a man of integrity. I pray he would continue to seek you, to serve you out of love and obedience.

Abba, there are just so many things rolling around in my mind. Obviously, I miss Emma incredibly. Is she worshipping you? I do thank you that she is with you, Jesus. Thank you for being her protector. Thank you for the love you have for her and that the room you prepared for her was ready.

Jesus, I just ask that you would continue to heal my heart. I just miss her so much. Please give her a squeeze for me and tell her that I love her more than my broken heart and sadness.

Oh Jesus, help me to look towards the future with hope. I've been so caught in the reality of living without her that I'm missing the reality that she is with you. I praise you for Emma and the life she did have on earth. I praise you for the love and joy she brought, and still brings, to my life.

Now I ask that you would heal me. My heart is still broken. Please mend it. I pray for hope and joy to reign in my life. Lord Jesus, take all of my cares and worries. Fill me with your peace. Strengthen and guide me. Tell Emma I love her...please.

Chapter 14
Things We Lost in the Fire

"Life is either a daring adventure or nothing. To keep our faces toward change and behave like free spirits in the presence of fate is strength undefeatable." Helen Keller

We'd moved into our first house...the blue one, the one that burned...in May of 1999. Bill and I had been married for two years. Together, we had three kids. Until two weeks after we moved in, when we found out I was pregnant. Our three-bedroom house suddenly seemed smaller...much smaller.

I couldn't wait to move. The townhouse where we'd lived for our first two years of marriage was shelter...but it'd been Bill's. It contained his stuff and only had two bedrooms...for five of us. Poor Matt got relegated to the unfinished basement. Kelsey and Dana shared a room with bunk beds.

I longed for a place of our own...my first house. Bill and I searched for months. We wanted to keep the kids in the same school district. Fortunately, that gave us a lot of options. But nothing felt right, nothing spoke...*I'm home.*

Not until the blue house.

We'd driven past it several times. It sat in the same subdivision where we'd lived, just on the other side. Never thinking we could afford it, we didn't check it out. Until one day our realtor said she had one more house to show us. She explained it was just in our range as the owners recently lowered the price. Were we interested?

Sure, we thought, might as well check it out. We had to do something. The townhouse exploded with the stuff of five people. And I needed to feel like the house was mine, too, not just his.

We drove back into our subdivision, having looked elsewhere at a few other houses. We turned...and I wondered. Could it be the house I secretly wanted? The one that caused my heart to beat every time I passed by? It was. We drove into the driveway and I turned to Bill. *We're home.*

In the blue house, the girls still shared a room, but Matt was upstairs near us, instead of in the basement. There was space, a huge yard...and it was ours. Mine. My very first home. A sanctuary for our merging family.

And then the news arrived. Another child added to our family. A true gift...the child to blend our family together, to belong to each one of us, and complete us.

Emma loved her home. I truly believe it was her favorite place to be...with her family and her pets. Jumping around the family room. Dancing in the kitchen. Eating mac & cheese at the table. Skipping up the stairs to find us when she felt alone. Playing in the yard. Emma's fingerprints were everywhere...and not just the dirty ones. That home truly belonged to her.

And now, just like her, it was gone. Destroyed by fire. Damaged beyond repair. The safety and security vanished. Annihilated. Not a square inch spared by the power of fire, the stench of smoke.

Even as I write, I feel awkward. How can I even think about the stuff...the things that were lost when Emma died? But I do. It was her home, too. So many memories lost. I suppose the stuff itself isn't all that important.

Or is it?

Growing up, my family moved a lot. Four different states by the time I was eight. A different house every couple of years. Fortunately, my stuff remained the same. I could bring it with me: my bed, my furniture, a sense of comfort in my books, a piece of calm with my toys.

As I grew and moved out on my own, many of those things came with me. Some became Kelsey's toys. Others were to give me that feeling of home...that place where I could live and breathe and grow. A sense of familiarity.

Now it was all gone.

The clothes from our kids' childhood, their toys. Our pictures. A stuffed animal I'd had since the day I was born. Bill's baseball collection. All of our books. My wedding dress. And the jewelry.

That thought devastated me the very first day of the fire. My grandmothers' rings, one from each side of my family. My mom's mom gave me her anniversary ring from my step-grandfather, the only grandfather I knew. Pappy. They'd just celebrated twenty-five years of marriage when he died. One of the last gifts he'd given to her. Now it was gone, forever.

And my dad's mom. A ring that belonged to her aunt...my great-great aunt. I remember Gram wearing that ring every time we'd gone to visit her in New Jersey. A beautiful filigree with an aquamarine...or blue diamond. Gram was never sure. It was irreplaceable.

I had that ring on the morning of the fire. Oh it was one of my favorite! A connection to my grand-mother, such a beautiful ring. Being a total girl, I took it off. It didn't match what I was wearing...a red Awana t-shirt, jeans, black hoodie.

Questions plague me...why did I take the ring off? Why didn't I keep wearing it...so I could continue owning it? Now I have no idea where it is. And I'll never find another.

Right or wrong I link so many memories to the things we owned. Pottery that belonged to Bill's mom...a lady I never met as she died two years before Bill and I met. His grandmother's dishes... the ones we used each time we had family over. A complete set of twenty-four...enough to use to serve Bill's large family...gone.

And so was my sense of security, of safety. So of-ten I'd go home, knowing all was well once in-side our house. Storms would rage but we'd all be safe. Rain could pour but not a drop touched our heads. People's words might hurt, but the comfort of home prevailed.

It took a while for me to feel safe again. To not think fire would follow me. I was afraid to cook. Even though the fire hadn't started because I used the microwave, there was still that fear...was it my fault? Irrational or not, it felt real. When we'd leave I'd unplug every appliance except for the refrigerator even though the fire wasn't an electrical one.

I felt displaced...disconcerted...exposed. There was not a single safe place to which I could retreat and recover and heal.

I hated the sight of fire, any type of fire. My heart raced and my breathing quickened at the barest glimpse of a flame...a wisp of smoke. Truthfully, some of those feelings still haven't gone away. They've diminished; I'm better able to control my reaction. But the smell of burning leaves on a crisp fall day no longer brings a smile to my face. The sight of leaping flames, whether in a fireplace or not, no longer draws me near to feel its warmth.

Some think I should be over that. I should no longer fear the effects of fire. They feel the focus needs to be on Emma instead of the things we lost. Some even believe the pain from Emma's death should be gone by now, too. I suppose they just don't understand, don't get it. I guess that's okay. Maybe one day they'll see; they'll experience deep sadness, overwhelming destruction. One day it'll all make sense.

I truly believe these feelings may never completely go away. I will always miss Emma, no matter how many years may pass. The events of the fire are now woven into the fabric of our lives. So much more was lost that day when fire destroyed our home. Yes, the worst was Emma's death. But the loss of safety and security threatened to complete the destruction. The loss brought such deep sadness. Not only from Emma's death...but not even having the things she enjoyed...her toys and memories, our tangible reminders. Memories become treasures. That's why I write. That's why I journal: to record and to remember, to allow my mind to return to times before tragedy struck, to try and breathe in fresh air.

It is with these feelings that I turn to God, that I seek him daily. My true safety. My true security. "Those who live in the shelter of the Most High will find rest in the shadow of the Almighty. This I declare about the Lord: He alone is my refuge, my place of safety; he is my God, and I trust him. For he will rescue you from every trap and protect you from deadly disease. He will cover you with his feathers. He will shelter you with his wings. His faithful promises are your armor and protection." (Psalm 91:1-4)

For while the fire took everything I held dear, and my life will never be the same, my heavenly Father promises there is absolutely nothing that can ever snatch me away...nothing that can separate me from his love. "No, despite all these things, overwhelming victory is ours through Christ, who loved us. And I am convinced that nothing can ever separate us from God's love. Neither death nor life, neither angels nor demons, neither our fears for today nor our worries about tomorrow—not even the powers of hell can separate us from God's love. No power in the sky above or in the earth below—indeed, nothing in all creation will ever be able to separate us from the love of God that is revealed in Christ Jesus our Lord." (Romans 8:37-39)

And it is in this reality, this blending of loss and love, faith and trust...missing Emma, yearning to see her again but waiting until heaven...living daily, balancing this truth so I can truly breathe...even amongst the ashes.

Appendix A
"Goodbye for Now"
Lyrics by Cindy Beier

Said goodbye to another one today
Who's gone up to heaven
I know that I'll see you again some day
But right now that doesn't matter
I cry hoping that the salty tears will hear my ripped
up heart
I pretend that if I wish really really hard I'll wake up
from sleep and you'll be here

I know you're with Jesus
I know you have the comfort that was lacking here
on earth
I know that you're singing with your hands raised
to a God
That you can reach out and touch

I know that you're happy
I know that your eyes will never shed another tear
I know that I'll miss you

Goodbye for now

There's no way to fully escape this pain
At times it's insurmountable
Yet through it all it's like God wrapped a blanket of
strength around me
He won't let go
Yet still I cry hoping that the salty tears will some-
how heal this ripped up heart
Then his peace washes over me and once again
I know

I know you're with Jesus
I know you have the comfort that was lacking here
on earth
I know that you're singing with your hands raised
to a God
You can reach out and touch

I know that you're happy
I know that your eyes will never shed another tear
I know that I'll miss you

You're singing
You're singing to a God you can reach out and
touch
I know that you're happy
I know that you're eyes will never shed another
tear

I know that I'll miss you
And I love you

Goodbye for now

Appendix B
Starting a Relationship with Jesus

"For God so loved the world that He gave His one and only Son, that whoever believes in Him will not perish but have everlasting life." John 3:16

As you've journeyed with me through this story of suffering and hope, it's my prayer that you're attention has been drawn to my Savior, Jesus. He desires to have a relationship with you, so much so that He gave His life for you. Please continue to read to learn what it means to have a relationship with Him.

Scripture is very clear of God's love for us. John 3:16 states that God loves us so much He sent a part of Himself—His own Son—so we can experience everlasting life with Him. All we need to do is believe and accept this free gift that He offers to us.

How do we do that? It's as simple as A, B, C.

The first thing we need to do is admit that we have a problem. And that problem is sin.

Scripture tells us "...for all have sinned and fall short of the glory of God." (Romans 3:23 NIV) Everyone sins...you, me, your neighbor, your pastor, every single person. Sin can be defined as things we think and say and do and, even don't do, that go against God's standard, His holiness. Sin creates a huge gap between us and God; a gap that we can't cross on our own no matter how hard we try or what we do. It doesn't matter how good we think we are, how often we go to church or even how much money we donate to needy people. There is absolutely nothing we can do on our own.

Think, for a minute, that you're standing on the beach. The Atlantic Ocean spreads out before. You're desire? To get to England. The first thing you do is try and get there...you jump. Your feet land in the water. Realizing the Atlantic is a little larger than you originally thought, you decide you need some force, so you back up a bit and get a running start. Sprinting at full speed, you jump at the last second, hoping the speed will propel you across the water. Unfortunately, you land only ten feet further than before. Determined to succeed, you decide to get some training. So you ask the gold medal winner for the long jump to give you tips. Soon you're ready to try again. You practice, you try again, you leap...and you fall into the water once more.

Yes, this is a silly thought. Of course there's no way for you to cross the Atlantic Ocean on your own. That's impossible. Truthfully, so is thinking we could somehow be good enough to come before the Creator of the Universe on our own.

You see, Scripture also tells us that sin has consequences, pretty severe ones. "For the wages of sin is death..." (Romans 6:23a NIV) God and sin cannot coexist. God is holy and perfect; sin is the absence of holiness and it's a horrible stench to God. Think of the absolute worst smell—week old garbage, messy diapers—our sin smells worse than that to a holy God. And God requires death to take care of the punishment for sin.

So the first step...tell God that you admit you sin. Tell Him about the things you've done or thought—the angry feelings or jealous words, the envy or hatred, the disregard for Him—He wants to hear from you. Admit that there's absolutely nothing you can do to get rid of your sin.

Then, the next step is to believe. God chose not to leave us in our yuck, our sin. He provided a way out for us...a free gift. Jesus. God sent Jesus, His Son, to earth as a baby. Jesus grew and lived an absolute perfect life. But He had one goal in mind...

the cross. Jesus knew that the consequence for sin was death and He chose to take that consequence we each deserve on Himself; He died a horrible death for you and me. "Christ suffered for our sins once for all time. He never sinned, but he died for sinners to bring you safely home to God. He suffered physical death, but He was raised to life in the Spirit." (1 Peter 3:18)

Jesus died so we might live. That's the rest of the story from Romans 6:23. "For the wages of sin is death, but the free gift of God is eternal life through Christ Jesus our Lord."

The final step...choose. Choose to believe that Jesus died, that He rose again and conquered sin and death for all. Choose to accept this gift and follow Him. Choose to trust Him, even if you're sure exactly how it all works. Choose to follow Him with your life. Your eternity depends on it.

If you sense that this is a decision you'd like to make, consider praying the following prayer. You can read it out loud or quietly in your heart...just let God know what you feel and how you'd like to respond.

God, I admit that I sin. I've done and said and thought things that go against Your standard, that dishonor and disobey Your commands. Please forgive me. I believe that You sent Your Son, Jesus, to take the punishment I deserve. I choose to follow You. I choose to live my life in obedience to You. Please reveal Yourself to me and help me become more like Your Son, Jesus. Amen.

Now, there's nothing magical about the words written in this prayer. But when you're heart genuinely desires to follow Jesus, you have access to the Creator of the Universe! He's the One who cast every star into place and made every fish in the sea... and He made you! "You made all the delicate, inner parts of my body and knit me together in my mother's womb." (Psalm 139:11) Life may not immediately change for you. Sin is everywhere and we live in a fallen world. But the same power that created every living thing in this world now resides within You. He knows you and He will give you the strength and power you need to follow and obey Him. "O Lord, you have examined my heart and know everything about me. You know when I sit down or stand up. You know my thoughts even when I'm far away. You see me when I travel and when I rest at home. You know everything I do." (Psalm 139:1-3)

Your next step? Get connected in a local church. Find one that teaches truth from Scripture, and believes Jesus is God's Son and the Savior of the world. Look for a community where you can learn and grow and ask questions. Don't go through life on your own; find a community of people who are striving to live following Jesus.

Spend time reading God's Word; His love letter to each one of us. The Bible is the best way to learn what He expects and how to live a life of obedience. Talk to Him, too through prayer. Share your hurts and feelings, your fears and failures, your hopes and dreams. Give Him all of you.

We're not perfect. Life is still hard and we still make mistakes. But God promises to forgive when we ask; He won't hold our sins against us when we tell Him we're sorry and truly desire to change our ways. "So now there is no condemnation for those who belong to Christ Jesus. And because you belong to Him, the power of the life-giving Spirit has freed you from the power of sin that leads to death." (Romans 8:1) But we can choose to trust Him even when it's hard...especially when it's hard. And then, one day, we'll find we're living in the truth of the following words: "Trust in the Lord with all your heart, and lean not on your own understanding. In all your ways acknowledge Him and He shall direct your paths." (Proverbs 3:5-6)

Appendix C
Things People Say

"The greatest thing a human soul ever does in this world is to see something, and tell what it saw in a plain way." John Ruskin

One of the most frequent questions I've been asked since Emma's death is how to respond to someone who has experienced the death of a loved one. The intent here is to provide insight into other ways to respond, of connecting. Because that's what it's really all about, isn't it? When someone is hurting, most of us want to reach out and help...to connect and encourage. To take a piece of the pain, no matter the circumstance, so it feels a little more endurable. "Share each other's burdens, and in this way obey the law of Christ." (Galatians 6:2)

As you encounter people in your life who have suffered deep loss, here are a few things you should know, and perhaps not say. Some of these comments listed were said to me or my family after Emma died. Some have come from my own mouth as I've tried to reach out to someone who is hurting. Some you may agree with, others you may not. That's okay.

As you read, you may find you've said these words. Don't despair....you may simply want to choose differently next time. The never-fail comment is to tell the person you have no words but just want him or her to know you care, that you're there. Silence at times offers more comfort than any spoken platitude.

You might not want to say:
How are you doing?

Why?
Honestly, you might not want to hear the answer. Or have the time to listen. And those in grief know that. We can identify those who are truly interested and those whose statement is a passing greeting, who don't really care to hear the answer. Besides, it all depends on the moment. One moment could be good but the next be deep darkness. There were times after Emma died and someone asked me that question, I wanted to scream: my life sucks! While in other moments great joy filled my heart.

Try instead:
How is this moment?

You may not want to say:
I know how you feel.

Why?
Each circumstance is different. No one can ever know exactly how the other person is feeling. Even when there are similar losses, the relationships with each person completely defines the loss. There may be similarities and, as a result, a connection. But remember, no two are alike.

Try instead:
I don't know how you feel but I'm sorry you're hurting.

———◆———

You may not want to say:
At least she went quick, or isn't suffering anymore.

Why?
While those statements may be true, the person is wondering why he or she had to die at all. The quickness of the death doesn't usually matter. The focus of the grieving person is now to figure out how to live life without the loved one. Lots of questions fill their minds. The reality that the person isn't suffering anymore may bring comfort to some, but there is still the pain and it's that pain that needs words of comfort.

Try instead:

I'm so sorry.

You may not want to say:
I'm going through a tough time right now, too. I just lost my pet.

Why?
Human life does not equal animal life, no matter how much a pet is loved. They're not the same. Period. And yes, this one was really said to one of my family members.

Try instead:
I have no words to say. I'm just really sorry.

You may not want to say:
God needed her or him more than we did.

Why?
That statement actually portrays an improper view of His grace and mercy. God doesn't *need* anyone like that. He chooses to have a relationship with us but doesn't need us to be in heaven with Him. He does have a plan for each of our lives and with that plan comes the time we will die. But saying those words really isn't all that comforting to the one left here on earth. It can cause God to appear uncaring.

Try instead:

I'm sorry. (Getting the point? Less is more....sometimes even a simple hug or gentle hand on the shoulder will speak louder than words.)

You may not want to say:
Now you're loved one has become an angel.

Why?
Okay, I may mess with some of you right now. We've made it this far so please hear me out. Scripture is very clear that we humans are created in God's image. "So God created human beings in his own image. In the image of God he created them; male and female he created them." (Genesis 1:27) Scripture is also clear that there are angels. I'm not disputing that. There is evidence of their existence all throughout Scripture. "Therefore, angels are only servants—spirits sent to care for people who will inherit salvation." (Hebrews 1:14) "Suddenly, an angel of the Lord appeared among them and the radiance of the Lord's glory surrounded them. They were terrified, but the angel reassured them. 'Don't be afraid!' he said. 'I bring you good news that will bring great joy to all people.'" (Luke 2:9-10)

What I'm saying is that we don't become angels when we die. "What are people that you should think of them, or a son of man that you should care for him? Yet you made them only a little lower than the angels and crowned them with glory and honor. You gave them authority over all things." (Hebrews 2:6-7) Angels have a very specific purpose "For he will order his angels to protect you wherever you go." (Psalm 91:11) "Praise him, all his angels! Praise him, all the armies of heaven!" (Psalm 148:2) When we have a relationship with Christ, we become heirs to heaven. We'll reign with Jesus for all of eternity and even judge the angels. "Don't you realize that we will judge angels?" (1 Corinthians 6:3) But I think the most compelling reason is that God sent Jesus to die for our sins; the angels did not receive the same gift of grace. "For God did not spare even the angels who sinned. He threw them into hell, in gloomy pits of darkness, where they are being held until the day of judgment." (2 Peter 2:4) "We also know that the Son did not come to help angels; he came to help the descendants of Abraham." (Hebrews 2:16) We are of such higher value than the angels.

Try instead:
Your loved one (important point....say that loved one's name) will be greatly missed.

You may not want to say:
Your loved one is now your guardian angel.

Why?
See last answer. Truth be told, I don't want Emma having the responsibility of watching out for me. I don't want her seeing me when I'm sad or hurt or

angry. I want her focus to be on worshipping Jesus. Again, you may disagree with me, and that's okay. But please check out what Scripture says and then decide if you'll believe all of Scripture or only parts of it.

Try instead:
Your loved one (say his/her name) will be greatly missed.

You may not want to say:
It's been three months, haven't you moved on by now?

Why?
There is no time limit to grief. Placing a time expectation like that, especially within the first year, is not realistic and may come off as uncaring and judgmental.

Try instead:
It's been three months. I still remember (insert loved one's name).

You may not want to say:
Nothing and ignore the person.

Why?
People need support after someone died. They need to know they're not alone because it definitely feels that way at times. They need to hear

people talk about the person who died, hear the name, share stories. While less is more, the important lesson here is to be quiet and listen, let the grieving person share if he or she wants to, but not avoid the person because you're aren't sure what to say. In moments of death, unless it's one of your family members, it isn't about you.

Try instead:
What's a favorite memory of (insert name)?

You may not want to say:
I don't want to bring up him or her because I don't want to make you cry.

Why?
Tears are healing. It's okay for people to cry. It's actually healthy and much needed. Tears may feel uncomfortable for you, and a little for the grieving person, but tears are good. The key is that you're asking! And listening! You never know the healing that can continue when you allow someone to cry.

Try instead:
Is this an okay time to talk about (insert name)? I wanted to share something with you about him/her.

You may not want to say:

I can't believe you said or did that? (Especially be-hind the grieving person's back)

Why?
Most anything goes after the death of a loved one...well, within reason. Unless you're a close friend, you should probably keep your opinions to yourself unless you're asked. This is not the time for proper etiquette. A grieving person's mind is often fuzzy; sometimes it's difficult to process all that's happening. Sure you don't want people swearing left & right or getting drunk or hurting someone but don't be surprised at what comes out. Just lis-ten. Don't judge. One day you could be in their shoes.

Try instead:
I'm sorry for your pain.

You may not want to say:
You know this is going to hurt.

Why?
Ummm...think about it. You're stating the obvious. It's very clear that life hurts after someone has died. That person was loved, had an impact in life, and loss hurts. The grieving person is well aware and doesn't need to be reminded.

Try instead:
I'm sorry for your pain.

You may not want to say:
You could always have another child.

Why?
One child doesn't replace another. If you have kids, do you feel the same way about each child? Of course not. Yes, you love all of your kids but each individual child is a special gift from God, unique and cherished. When one child dies, it's that particular child that is gone, and that place within the family that can never be refilled.

Try instead:
I'm sorry.

You may not want to say:
At least you have other kids.

Why?
Same as the previous answer.

Try instead:
I'm sorry your kids won't have their brother or sister to grow up with. Acknowledge the pain but don't try to fix it by pointing their attention somewhere else. There'll be time for that.

You may not want to say:
You'll move on, one day it won't hurt so much.

Why?

Because it's incredibly difficult to process and think of life without the person there let alone think that one day it won't matter, or hurt as much. Comments like this one just add to the pain. There's a sense that if a grieving person doesn't hurt, it's somehow disloyal to the one who died. While that is not true, there is a time and place for honesty by those closest.

Try instead:
I'm praying for you.

———

You may not want to say:
Time heals all wounds.

Why?
Time is neutral. It doesn't matter that the seconds tick on. Time doesn't influence anything; it's simply measurement to help us process events. Moving through grief takes incredible effort and conscious choices. Sure, there is the distance of time from the intense pain but I've met people who have lost a loved one many years ago and, after talking with them, you'd think it had just happened. It's what you do with time and your pain that makes the difference. And, truthfully, it's only through a relationship with Jesus that you can be truly healed.

Try instead:
I'm praying for strength as you journey through the pain.

You may not want to say:
At lease he or she didn't die like (insert any comparison).

Why?
Just don't compare. It's a form of judging one loss as worse than another. There's really no comfort in that. Death is death and pain hurts. Acknowledge their pain, not someone else's.

Try instead:
I'm sorry you're hurting right now.

You may not want to say:
Has it really been a year (or other time frame)? That went quick.

Why?
Time takes on a whole new dimension for those in grief. Minutes can feel like weeks and months are years. After Emma died, the day of the week was significant. I'd think, *last week on this day Emma died*. Then I'd move to months and finally, years. Saying the time went quick can feel like you're disregarding the pain suffered.

Try instead:
It's been a year? Wow. How is today/this moment?

You may not want to say:
God doesn't give you more than you can handle.

Why?
He does! I'm way over my head on this one. Living life after Emma's death, the fire, Bill's injuries and stroke is way more than I can handle on my own. The difference, and you may feel I'm picking apart words, is that on our own we can't accomplish much. But with God, all things are possible. (Insert reference) We can do all things through Him that gives us strength. (Philippians 4:13) That's the difference. I can't do it on my own but with God's strength and peace and guidance, I will continue on this journey until one day I will hear Him say: well done, good and faithful servant (Matthew 25:23).

Try instead:
I'm praying God will meet your every need.

Okay, one last thing, if you happen to catch yourself saying any of the comments listed above, don't despair. If you catch it in the moment, acknowledge it. For example, if "how are you" happens to slip out...say it. Catch yourself and maybe say, "Sorry. Life must be hard for you right now. How is this moment?" It's more important people know that you *care* and desire to be sensitive than if you catch yourself saying something you shouldn't. We all do it. Just move on.

And for those of us who grieve, remember this: people are going to say things that might hurt. Please don't be offended. Realize that they want to connect, to support you. Sure, there may be the occasional person who really doesn't get it, at all. And it kind of sucks that we're often the ones who have to extend grace but, as the Nike commercial so concisely put it....just do it. One day the shoes will be on the other feet and they'll learn...set the example for them. They might actually remember that one day.

About the Author

Kim Gunderson lives in the Midwest with her husband, Bill, and daughter, Kelsey. She's written for Christ Community in children's ministries for ten years and has had several curricula published with Big Idea, Inc. and David C. Cook. This is her first book. Kim currently leads Celebrate Recovery and Caring Ministries at Christ Community, sharing and teaching truth from God's Word, living transparently so others see an example God's faithfulness and sufficiency to meet every need.

6221514R0

Made in the USA
Charleston, SC
28 September 2010